THE FLYING PHYSICIAN WHO KEPT HIS PROMISE TO TANGIER ISLAND

BY

BILL LOHMANN

Author Bill Lohmann

Publisher
Wayne Dementi
Dementi Milestone Publishing, Inc.
Manakin-Sabot, VA 23103
www.dementimilestonepublishing.com

Cataloging-in-publication data for this book is available from
The Library of Congress.

ISBN: 978-1-7325179-1-2

Graphic design by:
Dianne Dementi

Printed in U.S.A.

Photo credits:
Front cover: *Bill Lohmann*
Title page: *Bob Brown/Richmond Times-Dispatch*
Table of Contents: *Bill Lohmann*
Last page: *Bob Brown/Richmond Times-Dispatch*
Back cover: *Bob Brown/Richmond Times-Dispatch*

For Barbara
Hope you enjoy
a visit to Tensis!

To my parents and in-laws —
Pete and Betty Lohmann
Cecil and Mary Little —
whose lives defined hard work,
commitment and love

Bill Lohmann

"Dr. Nichols was such a great, great man, and he saved so many lives. He loved Tangier dearly and was devoted to it. I hope this book will help people understand what Dr. Nichols meant to Tangier."

-- James W. "Ooker" Eskridge
Mayor, Tangier Island

"There is a reason Dr. Nichols was known as 'The Angel of Tangier Island.' He was a caring, compassionate man and an extraordinary physician who literally went the extra mile(s) for his patients. Staff Care was proud to select him as not just the Country Doctor of the Year, but the Country Doctor of the Decade."

-- Phillip Miller, Vice President -
Staff Care
Sponsor of *The Country Doctor
of the Year Award*

"Many pilots use their license to help others, but few contribute as much as Dr. David Nichols. For decades he used his talents in both aviation and medicine to give the people of Tangier Island access to healthcare and inspire many more to learn about how aircraft can connect and improve the lives of so many in communities across the country."

-- Mark Baker, President and CEO
of Aircraft Owners and Pilots
Association (AOPA)

"The story of the late Dr. David Nichols and his dream to care for the medical needs of the forgotten and beautiful people of Tangier Island is one for the ages. Bill Lohmann engages his razor-sharp journalistic skills with the grace notes of Southern storytelling to bring us *DR COPTR*. This unforgettable story chronicles Dr. Nichols' determination to serve the least of his brothers and remind readers of the difference one person can make in the life of another. Glorious and uplifting, this story will inspire you.Required reading for every Virginian and every citizen who embraces health care as a hopeful art as much as a healing one."

-- Adriana Trigiani
Author, Big Stone Gap

The Nichols family in the summer of 2017 (from left): Tom and Sarah with Truman and Juliet, Davy and Ivana with June, and Dianne.
Nichols family

Dear Bill,

Thank you for keeping your promise to David to write the story of his 30-year relationship with his beloved Tangier Island.

Through your dedicated pursuit of this project, my family and I have learned much more about David and those whose lives he touched.

As I read through these tales that you have so ably woven together, I can clearly see that David fulfilled his dreams because of the wonderful and talented people who were part of his life.

Thank you for creating a treasure for our grandchildren, Truman, June and Juliet. They will now be able to know the spirit of their grandfather who they believe is flying helicopters up in heaven.

You have captured the essence of my late husband, David Buell Nichols, and I will always be grateful.

Sarah, Davy and I thank you for the gift of this book.

With much appreciation,
Dianne

TABLE OF CONTENTS

Dr. David Nichols and Jimmie Carter speak to the crowd at the dedication of the new Tangier Island health center in August 2010.
Bob Brown/Richmond Times-Dispatch

PREFACE

This book so beautifully crafted by Bill Lohmann is a fitting tribute to my good friend Dr. David Nichols and the iconic community on Tangier Island. If you never had the opportunity to meet David this book will introduce you to this remarkable, caring man.

David and Tangier were perfect for each other. Tangier is an insular community where you need to earn acceptance, and they don't suffer fools gladly. David's solid stature and loyalty made him a beloved member of the island.

David was a keen observer, he knew how to diagnose complex medical problems and challenge those around him to strive for greatness. He taught us by example that there are no shortcuts on the road to meaningful accomplishment.

The David B. Nichols Health Center was built by and continues to be supported by the Tangier Island Foundation, which David and I started. It stands today as a legacy to this great man.

David died too early. I said at the time that I had never seen a man love a place with such a passion. When he was buried on the island next to the clinic, you could sense the closure. He was happy. He achieved what was most important to him: a life well lived, doing his best.

Jimmie Carter is founder and president of the Tangier Island Health Foundation.

Jimmie

Virginia Governor Tim Kaine, on the steps of the island's schoolhouse, visited Tangier in June 2007 to celebrate a $300,000 grant from the General Assembly that kick-started the fundraising campaign for a new health center.
Tangier Island Health Foundation

FOREWORD

Sen. Tim Kaine

As lieutenant governor, I traveled to the old medical clinic on Tangier Island for an official tour. I walked into the aging building that had seen better days and remember thinking, "This is the medical clinic?" It was basically a house with a leaky ceiling and floors that were really uneven. They were doing a lot of good medical care there, but I thought, "Wow, this is a pretty tough way to get medical treatment." It made a big impression on me.

I followed Dr. David Nichols' story over the years, and I was well aware of his unwavering devotion to the people of Tangier. But I had no idea about the conditions he was working under in that clinic. When I became governor, one of the goals of my administration was improved health care for all Virginians, so when my friend Jimmie Carter came to me and asked if I would include seed money in the state budget to help kick-start a fundraising campaign for a new medical facility on Tangier my answer was, "Yes, absolutely!" I knew the folks on Tangier needed it.

It was a great day when I went back over to Tangier in June 2007 to announce a $300,000 grant the General Assembly had approved earlier in the year. I remember the school children lined up at the dock to greet me as I arrived before we visited the site where the new health center would be built. The islanders were justifiably proud of what was to come, and David Nichols was too.

Tangier Island is a special place, and David was a remarkable person. It's one thing to provide medical care to a place and its people, but it's another to do it steadily and faithfully for more than 30 years. It strikes a chord in me whenever I see someone who has dedicated himself to others over a significant length of time. That's precisely what David did for the people of Tangier.

His motive was to help others, but like many helpers – and David was definitely a helper of the highest

Tim Kaine met with Dianne and David Nichols in February 2007.
Nichols family

order – it clearly meant a lot to him. I wonder whether he would have been able to do what he did for 30-plus years if he hadn't gotten such a feeling of satisfaction out of it. I'm sure it made him happy to know his life and his work meant so much to so many. When David died in 2010, I remember the headline on his obituary in the *Richmond Times-Dispatch* described him as "Tangier Island's angel." He truly was, and that's the way I always think of him.

I returned to Tangier in August of 2017, and it was exciting to see the health center in operation and to know that David Nichols' stories are still being told. He remains a living presence on Tangier today, and that's going to be the case for a long time to come.

Sen. Tim Kaine, D-Virginia, was first elected to office in 1994, serving as a city council member and then mayor of Richmond. He became lieutenant governor of Virginia in 2002 and was inaugurated as Virginia's 70th Governor in 2006. He was elected to the U.S. Senate in 2012. He was the Democratic nominee for Vice President in the 2016 national election.

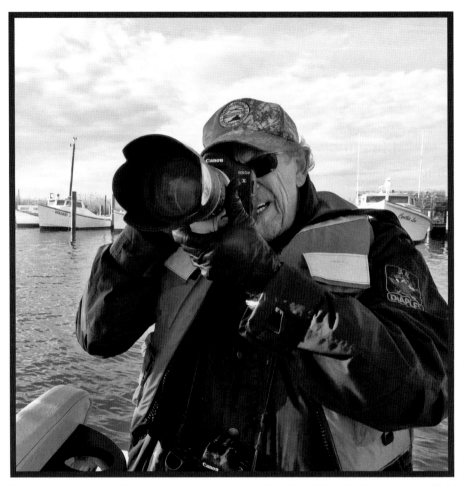

Photographer Bob Brown on assignment on Tangier Island in December 2014.
Bill Lohmann

THROUGH A PHOTOGRAPHER'S LENS

I first met Dr. David Nichols when Bill Lohmann and I caught a ride with him and his son, Davy, to Tangier Island for a look at the new health center that was under construction in August 2010. Davy was at the controls of the single-engine plane and the doc, who had been flying to the island for 30 years, was co-pilot. On arrival, we were greeted by the doc's protégé, Inez Pruitt.

After a look at the new facility, Dr. Nichols and Inez showed us the old clinic -- ceiling tiles falling down, wallpaper and plaster missing -- sort of a mess. At one point, the doc was telling us about the new health center when he suddenly began talking about his diagnosis of terminal cancer and how he would never be able to practice in the new facility. I photographed the moment he opened up to us about his situation, and it was a powerful image, a close-up of his face with a look that's hard to describe; sadness, yet joy that the new health center, a dream of his, would be fulfilled. (See Title Page)

With the help of Jimmie Carter, who had spearheaded the fundraising for the project, construction was put on a fast track and it was finished ahead of schedule so Dr. Nichols could attend the grand opening, which was held on the last Sunday in August in 2010.

On that day, the population of the island almost doubled as a huge crowd arrived for the ceremony. Bill and I flew over with Davy and U.S. Representative Rob Wittman and had to remain in a holding pattern for a few minutes as other aircraft landed. I counted more than 60 fixed-wing planes and helicopters, including then-Gov. Bob McDonnell's, lining the small runway.

It was announced that the health center would be named for Dr. Nichols, who also was awarded the "Country Doctor of the Decade" award. When he stepped out to wave to the crowd from the front porch of the facility, I stood behind him to show the size of the crowd. That shot remains one of my favorites. (See back cover)

I never saw him again after that historic event, but feel lucky to have met "Doctor Copter," and to have been able to record some moments in his life and the historic impact he had on the residents of Tangier Island.

Bob Brown, senior photographer for the Richmond Times-Dispatch, has been Virginia News Photographer of the Year three times and was the first photojournalist inducted into the Virginia Communications Hall of Fame.

Dr. David Nichols and physician assistant Inez Pruitt walk past a historic marker near the Tangier Island health center in August 2010. *Bob Brown/Richmond Times-Dispatch*

Nichols and Lohmann met in April 2010 when the physician flew Lohmann to Tangier to gather material for a story on the island. *Bill Lohmann*

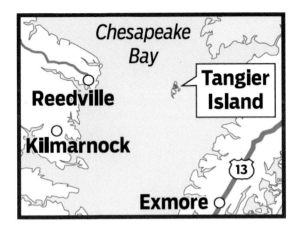

INTRODUCTION

Tangier Island is disappearing.

This speck of land in the Virginia waters of the Chesapeake Bay, rich in history and heritage and colorful characters, very possibly will not exist by the end of the century, perhaps far sooner. The low-lying island, Virginia's last off-shore fishing community, has been shrinking for years, a victim, scientists say, of rising sea levels, subsidence (the sinking of the island itself) and erosion. Whole communities on Tangier already are no more, homes lost to the bay and residents relocated to slightly higher ground on the island, or in some cases, to the mainland. The situation has grown more dire in recent years, and a 2015 scientific study said Tangier's hundreds of residents were at risk of becoming among America's "first climate change refugees." Without – or possibly even with – intervention in the form of a jetty, they might have only a few decades before the island becomes uninhabitable.

Map above: *Richmond Times-Dispatch*

Grim times indeed.

But the people of Tangier are a resilient bunch. They are no strangers to hardship and challenging circumstances. They have weathered hurricanes; imagine residing on a chunk of precious earth in the middle of the bay, no more than a few feet above sea level and barely a square-mile in size, and you begin to grasp the day-to-day courage required to live there. They have survived a loss of population and jobs and downturns in the fortunes of the seafood industry, the traditional source of their livelihoods as they work the bay waters for crabs, oysters and fish. Outsiders know Tangiermen, as the people of the island are called, for their cultural quirks: their distinctive dialect, reminiscent of their British ancestors and other isolated coastal villages along the East Coast, and the clusters of tombstones in many of their front yards.

But if you really want to know the people of Tangier, know this:

They are hardworking and humble and patriotic. They are deeply religious and unafraid to stay true to their beliefs, even when to outsiders it might not seem the most sensible thing to do; the islanders once turned down a Hollywood film project that would have brought much-needed income to their shores because the R-rated script left them cold. More than a dozen miles from the nearest mainland and sometimes seemingly pitted in an us-against-the-world stance, the people of Tangier always have turned to those they can depend on, those they trust the most: themselves.

They are proud and self-reliant, and when needed, defiant. This is one of those times. The science says they are doomed; their hearts say they can endure. They will not go down without a fight.

In a place like Tangier, the people are always on the lookout for glimmers of hope, signs that reward their faith and show them they are not alone.

Dr. David B. Nichols gave them such hope for more than 30 years.

Readers often ask, "How do you find good stories?"

I hesitate to respond "dumb luck" for fear of revealing a process dependent as much on serendipity as keen powers of perception, but that is the truth. The importance of being in the right place at the right time cannot be overstated or often accounted for.

In early 2010, I was hired by *Parade* on a freelance basis to write a piece for a series called "Our Towns." The idea, as I understood it, was to put together a piece on someplace or someone in Virginia that was off the beaten path, perhaps a little unusual, certainly interesting to a wider audience. I suggested several possibilities. The editors selected Tangier Island.

As a native Virginian, I've traveled the state fairly extensively on school field trips and family vacations. As a reporter for the *Richmond Times-Dispatch* since the late 1980s, I've had the opportunity to explore the commonwealth even more deeply, venturing down dirt roads and into mountain hollows that I otherwise would have had no reason to visit. For a long time, Tangier was a place that had eluded me, in part, I suppose, because it took some doing to get there. You couldn't drive there, of course, and unless you had a boat or some sort of aircraft, you were left with one option: a ferry. And even that wasn't altogether convenient since the daily ferry from mainland Virginia operates only during the warm-weather months.

I eventually traveled to Tangier for several stories, including one about the Tangier Combined School's annual prom. At the time, the school was one of only two public schools in Virginia with kindergarten-through-12th grades under the same roof; the senior class was 12 members strong. The prom was truly a community event. Townspeople turned out at the dock to cheer the prom couples in their fancy clothes and done-up hair as they boarded a boat for a hotel on the Eastern Shore of Maryland where they would dine and dance until after midnight. They returned to Tangier on a cruise across the pitch-black bay, changed clothes and fired up their scooters and golf carts for a scavenger hunt all over the island, passing bleary-eyed watermen on their way to work before dawn. Parents prepared breakfast at the school to cap off the affair.

When the Parade editors decided on Tangier, I began to think of a news peg on which I might hang the island's story. I immediately remembered Dr. David Nichols, the mainland family practice physician who also happened to be a pilot who had been flying to Tangier for many years to provide medical care. I'd read and heard of Nichols, but I'd never had the occasion to meet him. On my most recent visit to the island, I had noticed the early stages of construction of a health center. For a small island, such a project surely was a big deal, and Nichols, I'd been told, was the inspiration behind it. Seeing the island through the eyes of someone who had come to know and care for the people, I thought, would be a good way to tell the story.

I contacted Nichols, asking if I might be able to tag along with him on one of his weekly visits. He couldn't have been more gracious. He suggested we fly over in his helicopter on his day off so he could show me around the island and introduce me to some of the people he knew. I made the 90-minute drive from Richmond to his medical office in the town of White Stone, and he met me behind the building in an empty parking lot where he landed his four-seat helicopter. Before we departed, he had me slip on a life jacket, the type you would wear while paddling a canoe across a lake, and gave me the standard safety spiel about what might happen if we were to crash into the bay. All I could think of was the Paul Newman line in "Butch Cassidy and the Sundance Kid," in response to Robert Redford explaining that he couldn't swim and that's why he was declining the opportunity to leap off a cliff and into a river to elude a hard-charging posse. Newman laughed: "The fall'll probably kill you!"

We hit it off, but then Nichols struck me as the sort of man it would be hard *not* to hit it off with: soft-spoken, mild-mannered and earnest. We spent a fine spring day on the island where he introduced me to his sidekick and protégé, physician assistant Inez Pruitt. The chemistry between them was obvious, a professional rapport and friendship years in the making, an unlikely pairing in an unlikely place. They told me story after story, clearly enjoying the retelling, and remarking off-handedly they really ought to write a book. They took me on a tour of the health center, which had walls and a roof but was still under construction. We made plans to get together again in late summer, just before the grand opening, so I could do a piece on the medical facility for *The Times-Dispatch*.

But come July, Nichols called with news that was as awful as it was unbelievable: he had been diagnosed with metastasized cancer and had only months to live. He was only 62, and it was a stunner. The story of the imminent opening of the health center was still a story, but it certainly had a new, heartrending angle. A few days later, Nichols, with his son, Davy, piloting their single-engine plane, flew me and *Times-Dispatch* photographer Bob Brown to Tangier so we could put together a story-and-picture package in advance of the grand opening. I went back in August to cover the dedication of the center, a momentous and moving day. Over the ensuing weeks, as Nichols' health declined but his graciousness somehow strengthened, I grew to know him even better. He once again mentioned a book project, saying he'd wanted to write about his three-decade-long relationship with Tangier but never had the time, a commodity that now was slipping away. He asked if I would be interested in taking it on.

So, we set to work. I interviewed Nichols on several occasions as his health deteriorated, and I began talking to those who knew him best: family, colleagues and the people of Tangier who had come to view him as not only their physician, but as a brother. It was good I had so many other people to talk to because as a subject Nichols totally lacked the self-promotion gene. He had been the subject of numerous articles and television stories over the years, but those were other people's doing; he had generally gone along as a way to help Tangier. He never felt particularly comfortable talking about himself, which can be problematic for an interviewer.

"Well, I don't know what else there is to tell you," he said before we even got to lunch during our initial meeting to talk about the book and his life. He honestly thought we had exhausted the book-worthy details of his life – after an hour – and he worried that I would be unable to get enough material to write more than a few pages. What Nichols lacked in ego, his family and friends made up for with keen details and heartfelt observations of his life and work.

His family couldn't have been kinder or more accommodating in talking to me both before and after David was gone. They provided access to his papers, Davy flew me to the island, and the Nichols included me in family events – like the family dinner at Eckhard's, a German-Italian restaurant in Topping, situated across the Rappahannock River from the Nichols home in White Stone and across the road from the small airfield where Nichols maintained a small hangar for his aircraft. It had been one of his favorite dining spots. I felt a little awkward being there until his brothers began the meal by tossing hot rolls – actually *throwing* rolls – to everyone at the long table. If I had any doubts, I knew right then I liked this family. The meal went on for several hours with many stories and much laughter (and lots of rolls).

Through the course of this project, I came to know Nichols as a man intensely devoted to his wife, his family and to his patients, who worked long hours and operated with a single-minded dedication to perfection – that is, getting things done his way – that was certainly admirable but at times could be totally maddening. "A well-rounded workaholic" is how Dianne, his wife of 38 years, described Nichols as the three of us sat on their porch in October 2010.The project took far longer than I had expected, a combination of factors conspiring to divert my attention. The final product, I hope, achieves what I set out to do, which was not to deify David, but to tell a simple story of a genuine man with a good heart—and a nose for business and a love of flying – who found purpose and friendship in an unlikely setting: a small island a world away from anything he had ever known, where he saved lives and helped steel the residents as they fought for their future.

Bill Lohmann

Approach to Tangier Island.
Bill Lohmann

ONE

WAITING FOR THE DOC
'He's always teaching'

*O*n a blustery November Saturday, the wind blowing hard off the bay, Inez Pruitt drove her golf cart to the Tangier Island Airport, parked near the landing strip and waited. "Airport" is kind of a strong word for the facility: 2400 feet of asphalt airstrip surrounded by grass and dirt on the western edge of the island. There is no terminal or tower or any other structure, for that matter. But the airport represents one of the important lifelines to the outside world, allowing visitors to fly in for business or lunch and making it possible for residents to be plucked from the island in the event of emergencies and transported quickly to the mainland for medical care.

The airport also enables physicians to make house calls.

As Pruitt searched the sky for the helicopter piloted by Dr. David Nichols, she considered how glad she was that he was making a special trip to see a patient who had become ill but was refusing to leave the island for treatment. She also thought about how she dreaded, at least a little, having to face Nichols again.

Nichols was a physician who lived on Virginia's mainland and for years had made a weekly trip to the tiny Chesapeake Bay island – it was almost always Thursdays when he or someone from his practice would make the 15-minute flight to Tangier – to tend to the medical needs of its residents. The island had no resident physician, and Nichols had adopted the place and its people. Over the years he had been coming to Tangier, he had essentially become one of the islanders, no small feat in a place where wary residents welcome outsiders but hold them at arm's length, at least at first. Unless you live there and know well the joy and hardship of having a home on a fragile speck of land in the middle of the bay or you make your living on the water as generations of Tangiermen have done, you can't truly become one of them. Nichols had managed to bridge that divide.

However, he and Pruitt, at this point, were another story. Pruitt had worked for Nichols in the Tangier clinic for about a decade, learning the medical business from the ground up. A lifelong resident of Tangier, she was a high school dropout who had evolved from fetching sandwiches for the clinic staff to performing the duties of a nurse. She proved to be a fast learner and Nichols a good teacher. He taught her everything, including this: the patient always comes first. All of Nichols' expectations, demands and occasional barking intimidated Pruitt at first; she was terrified of him. But then she realized everything he did was for the good of the patient. Everything. He had a bad case of tunnel vision that manifested on occasion in outbursts directed at his staff, but it was nothing personal, she came to know, though that was a hard lesson to learn.

The more she watched Nichols, the clearer it became. She noticed the way he hugged the patients and held their hands and cried with them when the news was not good, the way he made house calls and didn't mind crawling into bed alongside the sickest of patients to simply comfort them. He spoke to patients in a kind but straightforward way, not holding back if unpleasantness needed to be discussed but not in a manner that would make matters worse. At a time when medicine was taking a less personal and more corporate approach, when physicians found themselves increasingly squeezed by business demands and time constraints, and patients began to feel like two-legged widgets on an assembly line, Nichols was a throwback. He took his sweet time when meeting with patients. Pruitt and anyone else who worked in his office confirmed this with immense admiration and a tiny measure of exasperation: as he conversed and consoled, counseled and cajoled, appointments were backing up in the waiting room.

Pruitt could see Nichols was much more than merely a physician who dropped into Tangier once a week to check a few pulses, write a couple of prescriptions and mend a broken bone or two. To patients, he was a trusted friend, a brother. This, she figured out, is what medicine is about: not just procedures, technology and information, but also compassion. Nichols seemed to have this in spades. For her, this had become not so much a job as an education.

"He's always teaching," Pruitt said years later. "He doesn't like to keep knowledge to himself. He loves to share it, and you just feed off that. He loves to teach, and he does it in such a way that you love to learn. His attitude has always been, 'The world should be a better place because one has lived. We're in this world to do something. Make it good.'"

Nichols and Pruitt made a good team, the willing teacher and the eager student, absorbing everything he had to offer. He saw in her considerable potential; she saw in him something to be emulated, a smart man doing something good for her beloved island. They were of one mind on many things; they came to be able to finish each other's sentences, to know, somewhat eerily, what the other was thinking. Neither objected to hard work, and both exhibited an unmistakable single-mindedness. They also shared another trait: stubbornness. Yet, Nichols had the upper hand. He was in charge, and from time to time he flashed a fierce temper, though usually all was forgotten and forgiven a few minutes later. Despite his propensity to occasionally blow off a little steam, Nichols was not a man known to hold grudges.

Pruitt eventually moved past being intimidated, but she tired of his occasional criticism and reprimands, which could be over-dramatic – such as the time she had neglected to order a supply of X-ray film, and the clinic ran out.

"I just want you to know," he blurted to her, "you've crippled the practice today!"

Because of changing personnel in the clinic and shifting assignments, Pruitt wound up doing a lot of lab work – drawing blood, processing it, analyzing urine samples. Important work, to be sure, but not what she enjoyed. She wasn't working as much with patients or with Nichols. "It was just so bland," she said. "I wasn't getting anything out of it." It also was a time of considerable personal stress as she was helping with her husband's boat-building business and managing a gift shop, as well as assisting her parents as they moved into a new house, tending to her aging grandmother and getting the clinic ready for a federal inspection. Worst of all, her sister-in-law was dying of cancer.

Pruitt didn't realize how unhappy she was at the clinic until she and Nichols had a difference of opinion over the use of a piece of equipment. Words were exchanged. She got angry and stewed over it. He wouldn't budge. Neither would apologize. She was totally fed up – for reasons not solely connected to the dispute – so she quit. She didn't just walk out, though; she gave him several weeks to find a replacement. Then she left in the spring of 1998. The months of summer dragged on, and the longer she stayed out, the more it looked like she would never return.

"He thought he was right, and he wouldn't admit he was wrong," Pruitt said. "I wouldn't admit I was wrong either."

Dr. Bob Newman, the other physician in Nichols' practice across the bay in White Stone who came to Tangier on alternating Thursdays, called Pruitt several times, trying to talk her into coming back to the clinic. Her sister-in-law died and her kids went back to school in the fall, and Newman told her returning to the clinic would be good for her and good for the practice. She did indeed return in the fall, but on those Thursdays when Nichols came to Tangier, it was clear to her the freeze between the two had not thawed, and she was convinced he was still angry with her.

"He would barely speak to me," she said.

Though, she noted that during the summer of her exile from the clinic Nichols called her when he acquired a new helicopter and invited her for a ride. In retrospect, perhaps he was extending a peace offering? They took off in the new helicopter, and Nichols landed nearby on an even smaller island, Port Isobel, home to an outpost of the Chesapeake Bay Foundation but otherwise uninhabited, and, Pruitt remembered with a laugh, "I really thought it was to kill me and hide my body there." It wasn't, and he didn't. But Pruitt was struck by the fact he remained angry at her for quitting the clinic.

"Out of the office, I was a friend, but in the office I made him so mad," she said, "Go figure."

Then came the breezy Saturday in November – after weeks of Nichols' cold-shoulder treatment since her return to the clinic – when Pruitt received a call from the adult daughter of a stroke patient on the island. Her father, who was already bedridden, seemed worse, and she didn't know what to do. Would Pruitt come by to check on him? The daughter thought Pruitt knew about all things medical since she worked at the clinic. Pruitt didn't, of course, but she was glad to look in on the woman's father. Pruitt checked his vitals and determined something wasn't right. She suggested the man would be better off in a hospital, which meant leaving the island, but the man was adamant that he didn't want to go.

Pruitt called Jean Crockett, a nurse who lived on the island but was away for the day, and asked for advice. Crockett told her she needed to call one of the physicians from the White Stone practice. And, she said, the physician on call that day was Nichols.

Ugh, thought Pruitt. Nichols might not have been the last person on earth she wanted to call that Saturday, but he was on the short list.

"I didn't want to talk to him," she said, "but the patient was more important than my personal feelings."

So, she took a deep breath, and she called. She explained the situation to Nichols. She suggested he call the family and insist the man be put on a boat to the mainland and a hospital.

"They'll listen to you," she told him.

No, Nichols said. He couldn't make a decision based on what she was telling him. "I'm flying over to see what's going on," he said. "Meet me at the airport."

It wasn't long before Nichols' helicopter came into view. He landed, walked over to Pruitt's golf cart and climbed in. The conversation was "cordial," Pruitt recalled, but nothing more. They reached the patient's home, and Nichols went to work.

As he examined the patient, Nichols reported his findings to Pruitt, and he started quizzing her about what that information might lead her to believe about the patient's condition. He systematically went through what could be causing the man's discomfort and included Pruitt in the process – just as he always had– pointing out this and asking that. It was just like old times, and she was reminded why she had loved the job she had walked away from.

Finally, Nichols told the family that he could not rule out a brain hemorrhage and he couldn't determine that without sending him to a hospital. But he also told the family it might not be a hemorrhage and that he was leaving it up to family members whether they wanted the man transported to a hospital, which was against the man's wishes and could, at this stage of his life, cause him more stress and suffering. Ultimately, the family elected against the hospital option. (The man's condition improved, and he lived several more years.)

Pruitt returned Nichols to his helicopter, and he flew home. That night, Pruitt lay in bed, sleepless, as the day ran around in her mind. She thought about all the knowledge she had gained from the house call to the ailing patient, and it suddenly struck her why she had grown so frustrated with her work that spring: she had stopped learning. She had simply been doing a job – lab work – and she hadn't been doing what she loved to do, which was working with patients and seeing to it that the clinic ran smoothly. Everything going on in her life outside the clinic had only compounded what was going on inside it.

So, the next week she talked to Nichols, and they reached an understanding, and she returned to doing the work she loved all along. "The understanding was silent," Pruitt said years later. "We just started back to working the way we always had prior to the 'disagreement.'" Neither apologized; each was too hard-headed for that. However, even though Nichols wouldn't say it, she could tell he wanted her back the way it used to be, and Pruitt wanted to be there, or as she put it, "I left because of him and returned because of him."

"I had missed it so much," she said. "I came back to loving my job. That's when I realized that's where I was supposed to be.

"I loved learning, and he loved teaching. In spite of us, we made a great team."

Snow day in Canada, winter of 1955 in Winnipeg, Manitoba, for the Nichols brothers: Peter on skis, Scott hanging onto the dog, John in the front of the sled and David in the middle. *Nichols family*

TWO

CHASING DREAMS
'A meticulous kind of guy'

David Buell Nichols came into the world on a bitterly cold day, as February days in Winnipeg, Manitoba, tend to be. The temperature in Winnipeg on Feb. 18, 1948, was 10 degrees Fahrenheit – and that was the high. Still, that would prove to be a relative heat wave compared to David's 18th birthday in 1966 when Winnipeg dipped to 49 below zero Fahrenheit. Nichols never harbored any fondness for the Canadian cold.

David was the third of four sons born to Peter Alexander Cunningham Nichols and Marion Blossom Buell Nichols. The two older boys, Peter and Scott, were born in Rochester, N.Y., where their mother grew up. David and John, the youngest, were born in Winnipeg after the family moved to Canada, their father's native country. Winnipeg is the capital and largest city of the province of Manitoba. Situated in Canada's heartland,

Winnipeg is midway between the Atlantic and Pacific
oceans, not more than a two-hour drive north of its nearest U.S. neighbors, Minnesota and North Dakota. It sits
at the confluence of the Red and Assiniboine rivers on
the eastern edge of the Canadian prairie and can trace its
origins to a trading post established in the 1800s by the
Hudson's Bay Company, which happened to be Peter
Nichols' employer.

Peter Nichols grew up in Newfoundland in far
eastern Canada, the son of an Anglican missionary who
tended, by boat, to the spiritual needs of several fishing communities. His given name was Alexander, but
he didn't much care for it or the shortened Sandy, so
he gratefully picked up the nickname of Peter, and he
made sure it stuck. When Peter was 12, his father died
of pneumonia, leaving the family in difficult financial
circumstances. Peter had grown up dreaming of becoming a physician, but after his father's death didn't have
the resources for a college education so he went to work
straight away after high school. He landed a job with the
Hudson's Bay Company, the oldest commercial corpora-
tion in North America that began as a fur trading business
and ultimately played a major role in the development of
Canada as a nation. In the dark days of the Great Depression, Peter, who turned 18 in 1932, was thankful for the
work.

He started as a clerk, but his apprenticeship didn't
last long as he quickly advanced to the job of full-fledged

fur trader and was given a territory in the wilderness of the Arctic region. He earned $15 a month at the beginning, became fluent in the Eskimo language and carved out a position of influence and respect among the native people. At one point he adopted an orphaned polar bear and kept it as a pet until it grew as big as he, and then turned it back into the wild. He spent five years traveling from post to post in the remote northern reaches of Canada, and on one of his journeys aboard a supply vessel he discovered an unlikely fellow passenger: a young woman heading home to the United States at the end of a graduation trip.

Marion Blossom Buell was the daughter of a prominent Harvard-educated attorney who associated with Rochester's elite, including George Eastman, who founded the Eastman Kodak Co. and revolutionized photography. The youngest of four girls, Marion enjoyed a life of privilege and opportunity that included enrollment in boarding schools – which she didn't much like – and then the chance to attend college, a not altogether common experience for a woman in the 1930s. After graduating from Duke University with a degree in English literature, her parents offered her a gift of a trip anywhere in the world. They expected her to choose a grand tour of Europe, as her sisters had when similar travel had been proposed to them. Instead, she elected to visit the Canadian Arctic, an odd choice, perhaps, for such a vacation, but not for Marion. She had fond childhood memories of visiting a family cabin on an island in northern Ontario, where she encountered pilots passing through who told wonderful stories of exploring the vast open spaces of the Canadian north, feeding her imagination and fueling her desire to journey there.

It took some sweet-talking on Marion's part, but she finally convinced her parents to let her go on a six-week adventure around Hudson Bay. Her father was so uneasy about sending his daughter alone into the wilderness that, unbeknownst to her, he hired a woman to ride along as a passenger on the boat and keep an eye on his daughter. Marion never knew about the family spy until years later, and she was furious when she did find out. No matter, while on the cruise she met Peter Nichols, and they hit it off as they sailed aboard the R.M.S. Nascopie, a World War I supply ship that had been repurposed to move passengers, cargo and mail for the Hudson's Bay Company. After going their separate ways, the long-distance relationship flowered over the coming months. They corresponded by slow-moving mail, difficult as it was in that day and in that part of the world, and on occasion Peter visited Marion and her family in Rochester. The unusual courtship culminated when Peter proposed marriage to Marion that Christmas – by Morse code over radio telegraph. She responded affirmatively, and the couple was married in August 1940 in a ceremony conducted in a familiar setting: on the deck of the R.M.S. Nascopie in Hudson Bay, as it was anchored just outside

Cape Smith, a busy port on the bay's northeastern shore where Peter was the new post manager for the Hudson's Bay Company.

Marion's family received details of the ceremony in a letter from J.W. Anderson, a Hudson Bay's district manager who stood in as father of the bride. Here are a few excerpts from the three-page, single-spaced typed letter, dated Aug. 7, 1940, the day of the wedding. It was a Wednesday.

Immediately after breakfast the saloon was prepared for the wedding ceremony. (T)he stewards re-arranged the tables in such a way that one of them acted as a temporary altar, with flags draped behind a silver cross in front of the flags, and a 'fair white linen cloth' covering the table. The hour for the solemnizing of the marriage was set for 10:30 a.m.

I had one last look around to see that all was in place and in order and then called on the bride. She looked altogether charming in her blue dress ... and a white prayer book in her hand. And I, you may be sure, was very proud to escort such a charming bride to the altar. The responses 'I do' were given in a quiet but quite audible voice by the bride and bridegroom, and when the question was put 'Who giveth this woman to be married to this man?' I answered in a firm voice, 'I do.'

Afterward came cake and photographs, according to Anderson's letter, and glasses of wine were raised in toasts to the happy couple. Then, later in the day, it came time for Marion and Peter to head ashore to Cape Smith.

Their motor boat, with an Eskimo crew, was standing ready to take them to their new home. Carefully the Eskimo crew held the boat to the gangway in the heavy swell to allow their new lady aboard. Then followed the bridegroom followed by a number of Eskimos who had been visiting the Nascopie. Then we saw the newlyweds standing on the deck of their boat surrounded by Eskimo friends. Everyone was jolly and happy and a merry banter was passing to and from as they were casting off from the ship. The assembled passengers gave them another three cheers ... and the last we saw of them was the tall couple standing on the deck of the motor boat waving their farewell in the midst of a group of short stocky Eskimos. We bade them farewell with full hearts and wished them all joy. And now they are alone in their new home.

So, with a simple "I do" Marion went from the familiar comfort of Rochester's high society to living as a newlywed at a frigid and distant fur-trading post.

In a letter home, Marion wrote of those first hours and days in Cape Smith and of the new world she was entering.

I used to wonder if the final good-bye to the Nascopie mightn't be sort of grim; but somehow it wasn't at all – perhaps because it all seemed so unreal, but mostly,

I guess because there was Pete standing beside me by the mast; and then, too, the much bigger good-byes to all of you had already been said long before.

They would spend two years in Cape Smith, where Peter, as the HBC's official representative, was viewed as far more than a mere trader. He was their link to an outside world they neither knew nor understood, and he was revered as a trusted friend of unmatched authority. As a result, he bore an unspoken responsibility, almost an expectation, to step in and do whatever circumstances required. That included traveling to a settlement of Eskimos struck by a fatal bout of food poisoning and burying the dead. When a physician was needed in a place that didn't have one, he occasionally was called upon. He once delivered a breech baby. Another time he was left with no choice but to amputate an Eskimo's badly injured finger; a medical professional who later examined the man's hand commended Peter's work.

Years later, Peter's stories of the rudimentary, emergency medicine he practiced in those rural outposts captivated young David and left an indelible impression, inspiring David to take up his father's unfulfilled career aspirations.

"Dave had a huge respect for our dad, probably more than any of the other brothers," said Peter Nichols, the eldest son, whose given name was Peter, unlike his father's. "I'm guessing that was in part because Dave was the sort of purposeful, organized, dedicated person that he was, and also because maybe he didn't pursue other influences quite as much as the rest of us. My sense was Dave was somehow less drawn by other things. By excluding other things, he tended to focus a lot on Dad."

Their father was "a pretty tough guy," having worked and traveled in rugged environments, often on his own, for so many years, said Scott Nichols. He learned to be firm, managing business operations from a great distance. Their mother, though "intellectual and artsy," Scott said, was tough in her own way, having carved out a life of independence, which surely seemed like rebelliousness to some, at a time when women didn't do such things. But once they married and began raising a family, Marion happily fell into the traditional role of mother and housewife that was so common in the 1950s and 1960s, although, as Scott recalled, she never lost her intellectual interest or independent thinking. Marion had inherited a sum from her family, but she and Peter decided to use the money for educating their sons, not for lavish vacations or other gratuitous pursuits.

"She was better educated than my father, but there was never any tension between them over that," Scott said. "Just different roles. She ultimately was a subordinate, dutiful wife, but my dad gave her the latitude to be the person she wanted to be and was. They were a good team."

The Nichols brothers with their father in 1994 at John's cottage on Lake Ontario. David is at the bottom of the photo, sitting in front of his father, Peter. John is directly behind his father, Scott to his left and Peter is at the top. *Nichols family*

The family had settled in Manitoba after Peter took a job in the Hudson Bay Company's Winnipeg office. Over the years, the Nichols family lived in a series of three homes, each successively larger and all on the shores of the Red River. David remembered the last one best; he turned 7 the year they moved into the two-story house on South Drive. It was a comfortable house in a nice neighborhood with a lawn that sloped down to the river. In the winter, the boys would toboggan down the snow-covered hill and skate on the frozen river, although years later when describing his hometown David remembered not so much the fun as the bitter cold of the place.

"I hated the weather with a passion," he recalled. "Could not stand it. I wanted to get out of there as soon as I could." But, he added, "The people were nice, the education was superb and I loved my parents and my brothers."

Despite the cold, David and his brothers enjoyed happy, contented childhoods in a house where they learned about commitment and loyalty and devotion to task – their father worked for Hudson's Bay Company for more than 40 years – and doing things the right way. Before heading off as a teenager to a summer job in the Arctic, Peter, the eldest, recalled these parting instructions from his father: "Don't disappoint me." Those words resonated with him always.

David was the quietest of the brothers, the shyest, the most reserved, perhaps the most concerned about how others viewed him and the most sensitive to the feelings of others. Amid the bounty and mild mayhem of Christmas mornings in the Nichols household, David, in stark contrast to the ripping open of packages by his brothers, would methodically and appreciatively unwrap one present at a time, play with it for a time, and then move on to the next. His brothers said he also was the most intense, the best-behaved and his room was always the neatest. "A meticulous kind of guy," said his brother Peter.

David often was drawn to solitary pursuits. He embraced distance-running before it became widely popular among the masses, and in a nod to his Scottish heritage, he learned to play bagpipes, an instrument seldom associated with popular music and one whose doleful sound has a tendency to keep crowds away. But bagpipes appealed to David, and he became good enough to serve as pipes major for his school's cadet band, often practicing as he walked back and forth along the shore of the Red River behind his home.

"I remember one time I was playing along the river bank and in the distance I could hear someone piping back the same thing I piped to him," David said.

He was the least-inclined of the brothers to be free-spirited, Peter said, but that didn't mean he was above living a little on the edge. His father forbade the brothers from riding motorcycles, but his edict apparently didn't prohibit the boys from building a motorcycle from scratch with spare and improvised parts, which David did. He bought "a pile of junk for 10 bucks," Peter recalled, and using such mechanical ad-libs as a coat-hanger for a brake cable and pilfered corks from liquor bottles for the clutch, he got the thing running. Violating their father's rule, he and youngest brother John took the bike out for a spin one night. To make it appear legal, the teens found an old license plate and tried to paint it to match current-day plates, but their mother's pastel paints were slow to dry so the plate was still wet when they went riding. They rode on the shoulder of a road, heading the wrong way, in the dark, with a burned-out headlight. It almost goes without saying a police officer stopped them, but they got off with a warning, perhaps because of their youthful ineptitude, and John was left with an impression that he was glad to share with David's wife and children many years later: "David was not a good criminal."

The Nichols boys attended St. John's-Ravenscourt School, a prestigious, private boys school about a mile from their home which has produced 18 Rhodes Scholars over the years (and began admitting girls in the 1970s). Their parents placed a high value on the boys' education – Peter from what circumstances denied him academically and Marion from what she gratefully experienced – and the boys, though afforded a large measure of independence, clearly understood what was expected of them. As children, they might have dreamed of being a truck driver and their parents would have been supportive, as David said, but they'd better plan on becoming the best truck driver imaginable – with a college diploma tucked in the glove compartment. Their parents would insist on it.

Considering the varied and successful career paths taken by the brothers – Peter became a banker who worked at the World Bank, Scott a lawyer and major general in the U.S. Air Force, and John ran his own civil engineering firm – it might seem preordained that David would have gone into some highly challenging field. But no one would have imagined that result in the 1950s and early 1960s when David was a boy just trying to find his way.

"Where the rest of us got there by goofing off or winging it," said his brother Peter, "David succeeded by persistence and hard work."

His brother Scott believes David became such a good doctor in large part because he worked hard to achieve what he did. "He had a definite empathy for people who struggled and worked hard, for whom things didn't always come easy and were willing to apply themselves."

David's interest in medicine undoubtedly originated with his father's unfulfilled dreams, though neither he nor his brothers could recall precisely how it was specifically nurtured and grew into his professional calling, but it was just one of a pair of long-range ambitions that bubbled to the surface during his childhood. The other was aviation.

The boys made model airplanes, as boys in that era often did, and Scott could recall how he and David were mesmerized by a local television station's nightly sign-off that included footage of a soaring U.S. Air Force jet. Little boys never forget stuff like that. Their father, of course, often returned home with stories from his flights to the Canadian north, and the boys themselves occasionally were passengers on planes that carried them to visit family back east.

But one thing that really brought home the notion of flying to David – and the concept that piloting one's own aircraft was not so wild a dream – was a neighbor who piloted his own floatplane. David often watched in admiration and awe as the neighbor would return home, landing his plane right in front of the Nichols' house on the Red River.

"I always thought that was neat," David said. "I liked all things to do with flying."

In fact, David proudly recalled years later a test administered in high school to determine students' aptitude for possible careers. The two fields David scored highest in? Medicine and aviation.

If the long winters in Winnipeg meant harsh weather and less-than-pleasant times in the classroom, the summers represented something else entirely for David: pure, carefree fun. When spring arrived, their father traveled for weeks or even months at a time in the thawing north to reach the far-flung trading posts that were inaccessible in the winter. The boys, who enjoyed dual citizenships by virtue of having a Canadian father and an American mother, spent summers with their mother's family, either at a remote cabin in northern Ontario, or more often at the large home of their maternal grandparents on on the southern shores of Lake Ontario in western New York.

The place was overrun with cousins and aunts and uncles, as well as several dogs, and one summer a dozen or so ducks that roamed around outside and resided in a garage. The boys enjoyed a degree of freedom that made their visits seem like a combination family reunion and endless summer camp adventure. Perhaps even more than his brothers, David came to appreciate those summer getaways to the lake – the laid-back atmosphere and the warm embrace of family – as a most welcome change of pace.

"It was just nice to get away from all the hassles of the cold weather and be with our Rochester family," David said.

Those summer vacations fostered a deep camaraderie among the large, extended family; David loved picking up the phone in later years and calling one seldom-seen cousin or another just to chat them up and see how things were. At the lake house, there was, of course, swimming and boating and a whole host of other predictable activities, but there also were part-time jobs to be had – David worked three summers as a lifeguard – and household projects to be tackled. His brothers fondly remembered a shelter that David decided he would build to accommodate the trash cans. He spent many hours painstakingly constructing it, using only the finest materials and the greatest care. He turned the assembling of a simple storage space for garbage cans into an endeavor that resulted in a veritable lodge featuring a roof and the sort of structural reinforcement that could withstand an assortment of natural disasters. Those who knew David best said this episode foreshadowed his involvement in bigger building projects years later.

"This was built," his brother Scott recalled with a laugh. "We've joked that it's probably still there because it couldn't be destroyed. This thing was built and over-built and built some more. It was beautiful. But it was typical Dave. He liked things done well – and solid."

When it came time for college, David headed away from the cold of Winnipeg and straight toward the part of the world where he was completely at ease, a place that held so many happy memories for him: western New York. He attended Hobart College in Geneva, a small private school in the Finger Lakes region of the state, less than an hour's drive from his grandmother's home in Rochester. He decided to pursue medicine as a career, and majored in biology at Hobart, graduating in 1970. He then returned north of the border to Montreal and McGill University, one of Canada's finest, and earned a master's degree in anatomy, building his academic record, nurturing faculty connections and continuing to develop a much-needed confidence that had sprouted at Hobart so that he could eventually enter medical school.

He told a funny story on himself in later years – related by Allan Riggs, a physician assistant who worked for Nichols in the early 1980s – about an important interview for medical school that didn't get off to the best start. Nichols walked into the office of the professor who was leaned over reading and said something to the prospective student that was either not enunciated well or heard incorrectly.

"You feel old?" Nichols asked somewhat confused, repeating what he thought he had heard.

No, the professor said, "My name is Phil Gold."

Oops. Not exactly the sort of introduction you want to make when you're desperate to persuade someone you're worthy of admission to medical school. Nevertheless, Nichols pressed on and must have impressed sufficiently. "It obviously was not a negative event since he went onto med school at McGill," said Dr. Phil Gold, in an email in September 2013. Gold, a professor of medicine at McGill and executive director of the McGill University Health Centre, did not recall the episode, but said it was entirely possible. He talked to a lot of students in those days in his roles as an instructor and as a member of the admissions committee.

What is telling is that Nichols remained undaunted by the incident, the sort of thing that might have derailed him in earlier years.

"In his college years, he came out of his shell," Scott said. "By the time he got to McGill, I think he was up and running and had a plan. He kind of knew where he was going, he knew what he wanted to do and he was his own man."

During his second year in the master's program, David became president of the Post-Graduate Students' Society at McGill, a leadership position that would have seemed out of character a few years earlier. The organization, which arranged events and activities of interest to students, met in one of the many old stone houses that surrounded the university in the heart of downtown Montreal, and was made up of representatives from various disciplines. It turned out to be a most beneficial exercise for David, not only for the experience he gained operating as a first among equals but also the connections he made, the most notable of whom was a representative from the nursing program named Dianne Louise Robertson. From Victoria in western Canada, Dianne had watched and listened as David conducted meetings, but didn't meet him until the group's Halloween party in October 1971.

"I have a vivid memory of David surrounded by a group of students, talking about all sorts of things," Dianne said. "I do remember thinking that he seemed like a pretty nice guy. I think it was apparent even then that he had a unique ability to draw people out."

Later that evening they got a chance to talk, and Dianne laughingly recalled how David unwittingly became something of an experiment. In class, she had been learning techniques for interviewing patients, so she decided to practice on him.

"I interviewed the devil out of him," she said. "Nobody in his entire life had asked him so many questions about his life. It worked like a charm."

David was smitten, and so, too, was Dianne. On their first date, David took her to see a new film, "Fiddler on the Roof," at one of Montreal's premier movie houses. Another evening, he took her to dinner at a rooftop restaurant. He won her over, but they didn't always visit the finest places: Dianne spent many of their getting-acquainted evenings typing rough drafts of his master's thesis. Typing never was one of David's strong suits.

In January, barely two months after their first meeting, David proposed marriage. They became engaged on Jan. 15, and, proving he was a romantic at heart, he brought Dianne flowers on the 15th of every month leading up to their wedding in July. That spring, David was accepted into the Faculty of Medicine at McGill, Canada's oldest medical school. He would begin classes in

September, but he and Dianne had business to attend to before then.

In June 1972, they left Montreal and headed west, stopping in Winnipeg to visit David's parents and then tent-camped their way to Dianne's home on Canada's west coast in Victoria, British Columbia. "Saw lots of bears!" Dianne recalled years later. They were married in July in the small church that Dianne grew up attending; the reception was held in her parents' backyard. They then drove back to Montreal, making a stop at David's grandparents' house on Lake Ontario, and arrived at McGill in time for classes – David in his first year of medical school, Dianne in her last year of pursuing a bachelor's degree in nursing.

John C. Bray was working at Montreal General Hospital while he applied for entrance into medical school. On his lunch hour, he took a physiology course down the hill at McGill's McIntyre Medical Building where he became friends with classmate, Robert Johnston, who also was applying for medical school. Johnston used to speak favorably about a graduate student who was teaching an anatomy lab and who also was trying to get into medical school, a young man by the name of David Nichols.

"Needless to say I heard the name Nichols mentioned time and time again by Bob during that year,"

Left - David and Dianne were married July 22, 1972, in Dianne's hometown, Victoria, British Columbia. *Nichols family*

Bray recalled. "Thus when I found out that the three of us had gotten into medical school I was anxious to meet the mysterious Nichols character which I did on the first day of school. We talked at lunch on the balcony of Beta Mu Medical fraternity house and never stopped talking for the next four years."

During David's first two years of medical school, he and Dianne lived within a block of the McIntyre Medical Building in an apartment that Bray said became a gathering spot for friends who enjoyed games of Monopoly and Risk, listened to Neil Diamond's "Jonathan Livingston Seagull" (a Nichols favorite) and drank Harvey Wallbangers, a popular cocktail of the day. Dianne, having arrived in Montreal as a registered nurse, obtained a bachelor's in nursing at McGill, worked at Montreal General and later taught nursing at Vanier College. During David's third year of medical school, the couple moved to an apartment in the Montreal suburb of Mount Royal to be closer to Vanier and Dianne's teaching job. Bray lived with his parents nearby, so he and David drove together to school. In their third year of medical school, Nichols and Bray worked in internal medicine at Montreal General. Mondays were particularly bruising days as they ended with rounds and case presentations with the chief of medicine, who was "well known to eat medical students for lunch," Bray said.

"Knowing about these days, my mother would always serve me steak and fries for supper," Bray said.

"Anyone who knew Dave Nichols knows he considered beef a food group unto itself, and I remember how he called me one Monday evening and inquired as to what I'd had for supper. I replied that being Monday, of course, it was steak and fries." David was dismayed. Dianne was taking cooking classes, Bray said, and the Hawaiian pork chops she had prepared didn't stack up well, in David's mind, compared to Bray's steak.

Nichols loved hamburgers. He claimed to have eaten 16 in a day during his time in Rochester, and he and Bray would often grill burgers on his apartment balcony – in violation of a local ordinance, so they cooked while keeping a watchful eye for police. Although financially strapped as medical school students, Nichols and Bray occasionally would visit Joe's Steak House in Old Montreal and splurge on rib-eye steaks, fries and Coca-Colas, a filling meal for $5. Mr. Steer, another Montreal institution known for excellent burgers and curly-Q fries, also was a Nichols favorite.

"Doctor or not, dietary advice (and) cardiovascular risk notwithstanding, nothing could keep Dave away from his beef and fries," Bray said.

David and Dianne's first child, a daughter, Sarah Buell Nichols, was born in October 1975 in Montreal. The following spring, David graduated from medical school. The young man had certainly had found his way.

"He blossomed," said his brother Peter. "McGill for David was a breakout. He was on top of the pile, and we were incredibly proud of him."

As David and Dianne readied to leave Montreal in May 1976 and begin a new life, they cleared out their apartment and sold furniture and other items. His friend and classmate Bray joked that the experience showed him how much David truly valued each and every dollar.

"Dave bunched up groups of half-used, occasionally slightly chewed pencils and sold them for 25 cents," Bray recalled, "and they sold!"

On graduation day, David, Dianne and baby Sarah, along with David's parents, left Montreal in a van driven by Scott, and headed for Virginia. David was about to begin his three-year residency in family practice at Riverside Hospital in Newport News, a city in southeastern Virginia on the James River as it flows into Hampton Roads, one of the world's largest natural har-

bors. David had always heard med school graduates should do their residency in a place where they plan to practice, and Virginia was the place he and Dianne settled on because

Nichols graduated in May 1976 from McGill Medical School in Montreal, Quebec. *Nichols family*

David's parents had retired to a quiet, waterside home on the state's Northern Neck, a pretty wedge of land etched with creeks and bordered by two rivers (the Potomac and the Rappahannock) and the Chesapeake Bay, roughly an hour's drive from either Washington D.C. or Richmond. His parents liked the water and the moderate climate – compared to Canada – and David liked those things, too, as well as the personality of the place. Relaxed and rural, the Northern Neck is largely farms and forests, interrupted by small towns that exude an authentic charm and a rich sense of history. Native American tribes were the original inhabitants before being pushed aside during colonial times for the creation of tobacco plantations in the early days of America. The Northern Neck was home to founding families, such as the Washingtons and Lees, the origin of its nickname "Athens of the New World." George Washington, who was born on the Potomac side, described The Northern Neck as "the Garden of Virginia." President James Monroe was born there, too.

The Northern Neck's population is racially and economically mixed – from hardscrabble to well-to-do. The Northern Neck long has beckoned weekend residents and well-heeled retirees, all seeking a laid-back respite on the water from the workaday world. Residents and frequent visitors report an immediate and dramatic drop in stress and blood pressure once they cross one of the bridges onto The Northern Neck, or can no longer see Interstate 95 in their rear-view mirror. The Northern Neck is a place where they can lose themselves in the countryside, meandering past roadside vegetable stands and historic churches, browse an antique shop, get a fine lunch in a restaurant that used to be gas station, or find a quiet spot deep in a nature preserve and search the sky for eagles. David had developed this notion that he'd like to be an old-time doctor in a modern age, and this seemed like the sort of place where he could chase that dream.

"I always wanted to do that," he said years later. "I don't like to live in cities. I really like the country life-style. I like doing house calls. I consider it a venerable institution, the practice of country medicine."

David went to work in 1979. The White House was occupied by Jimmy Carter, a man who endured a turbulent four years in office but whom David would come to admire for the worldwide charitable work he performed after leaving Washington. David greatly respected that sort of devotion to helping others, but in the summer of 1979 he was a young doctor with a growing family and a new practice, and his focus was on building a successful business.

In August, he set up his family practice in White Stone, a small town with a population of about 400 and one traffic light on the Rappahannock side of the Northern Neck, a one-doc shop with a nurse and an office assistant. He purchased a medical building that had been vacated by physicians who left to work at a new hospital in the nearby town of Kilmarnock. He didn't have any local competition in the area of family practice, but the lack of competition didn't ensure success. The costs of starting a solo medical practice are steep, and David took his financial obligations seriously, so at first he moonlighted on weekends at the emergency room of the Kilmarnock hospital to make extra money. Though his time was stretched, he also began thinking about how he could do something more community-minded beyond his usual office hours and hospital work.

"I feel like when you're given a medical education, that's a real gift," he said. "You should share that with people to show thanks, give some of that back."

That's when Tangier Island came into play.

Tangier harbor.
Bill Lohmann

THREE

Wanted: Physician
'Don't leave us'

*T*o say Tangier Island is small is to speak the undeniable truth. The island is just more than a square mile
in size, though only a fraction of it is actually inhabitable.
Fewer than 500 people live on the island, their homes
on three distinct ridges, separated by tidal streams and
marshes connected by footbridges. Most of the low-lying
island is barely above sea level; according to a 2016 pro-
file of the island prepared by the Accomack-Northampton
Planning District Commission, the highest slope on Tangier is six feet above sea level. Marshes represent the vast
majority of what's left of Tangier, which is significantly
smaller since Captain John Smith and other English
explorers "discovered" the island in 1608. Long before,
local Native Americans used the island for hunting and
fishing. The first English settlers raised cattle. Tangier

today has no livestock, though there is a significant herd of cats that roams the island.

Looking at the small island now, after the bay has overtaken much of its land, it's hard to imagine it as a site of ranching operations. Homes line narrow lanes. Many front yards feature clusters of tombstones, land suitable for burial being in such short supply on the island. The water table is so high, the vaults cannot be buried at a standard depth so the lids of the vaults are typically visible.

Graves in front yards always grab the attention of visitors, who also are generally enthralled by the distinctive dialect spoken by Tangiermen, many of whom descend from English settlers that arrived generations ago. There are few cars and trucks on Tangier, the need for such being minimal and there being nowhere to drive anyway. Bicycles and golf carts are popular modes of transportation – or just plain, old walking.

Since the days of raising cattle on Tangier, the people of the island have depended on the bay for their livelihoods – catching crabs, tonging and dredging for oysters, and fishing – leaving them at the mercy of the whims of nature and men, the latter in the form of well-meaning government regulations. But working the waters is what their ancestors did, so that is what they do. Tradition dies hard on Tangier, where the people are at once adaptable and obstinate.

The island has a few restaurants, a single market and a pair of bed-and-breakfasts. The island has no banks, but one ATM. Cell phone service is unreliable, and alcohol is not for sale on the religiously conservative island, although no one objects if you bring it with you and enjoy it discreetly.

Advancements in communication have made Tangier less secluded than it once was, though you still need a boat or an aircraft to get anywhere else. The island is about 15 miles from both Virginia's Eastern Shore and its western shore. It's within a half-dozen miles of the Maryland state line, and the only year-round daily ferry serving Tangier runs to and from Crisfield, Md. Virginia ferries operate seasonally.

It was in the mid 1970s when David Nichols was introduced to the island. During a summer break from medical school in Montreal, he and Dianne visited his parents on the Northern Neck, and they traveled across the bay on a family boat trip to spend the day on Tangier.

"They didn't have a doctor," Nichols recalled years later, "and I think my wheels started turning then."

He never forgot Tangier, and the wheels of interest began turning with even more purpose after an experience during his third year of medical residency in Newport News. Dianne's parents had come from western Canada for a visit in October 1978 to celebrate Sarah's third birthday. When he drove them to the airport for their flight home, he spied a sign advertising $10 introductory flight lessons. He signed up, took his first lesson that month and learned to fly single-engine planes. The following summer he completed his medical residency, opened his practice and neared the completion of his pilot's training, finding himself on the verge of fulfilling the double-barreled prophecy of the long-ago aptitude test.

As he settled into practicing medicine solo in what became known as White Stone Family Practice and worked weekends in a hospital emergency room, he kept thinking about Tangier, how the island lacked a resident physician and how much he liked the simple beauty of the place and how it could be a perfect fit now that he could fly himself over there. So, he picked up the phone and called the Tangier mayor, Robert Thorne. What Nichols didn't know – or didn't remember years later – is that the town was in the process of advertising for a physician in area newspapers. Thorne was receptive to Nichols' interest, but he also told him, as Nichols recalled, "If you come, you've got to stay. Don't leave us." The island had a long, sometimes strange history of physicians coming and going, and it was looking for a firm commitment, not just someone who wanted to feel good about themselves for a few months and then lose interest and move on.

Nichols traveled to Tangier on Nov. 1, 1979, according to his pilot logbook, and met with Thorne and the town council. "A wonderful discussion," recalled Thorne. "He seemed to have a tremendous knowledge of medicine. Not only that, he loved people. You could tell that by the way he would reply to questions." The island received no other replies to its ads, which, as Thorne said many years later, could have been viewed as a disappointment, "But all we needed was one."

And Tangier got its one.

So, the announcement of the new physician was made in a town council meeting but also at Tangier's two churches, where more islanders were more likely to be in attendance. "Everybody was so delighted," Thorne said.

Skeptical, but delighted.

Nichols recalled being taken aback by a conversation with Helen Jane Landon, a nurse-midwife and native of Tangier who had served the island so well after returning from mission work overseas. She beseeched him not to betray the trust of the Tangier people but also predicted he probably would. "You're going to leave just like the rest of them," Nichols recalled her telling him, "and then they're going to be stuck alone again."

"I'm not going to do that," Nichols told her. Many years later, he recalled Landon's doubt in his longevity, saying with a laugh, "That might have more than anything kept me doing it."

However, he admitted he didn't really know what he was getting into when he agreed to travel to Tangier once a week.

"I just knew there was a need. I liked the island, and I liked the combination of a little flying with it," he said. "My dad encouraged me all along the way. He always said, 'David, don't give up Tangier.' He was very influential all my life, and he wrote the book on loyalty. A very loyal guy."

A constant medical dilemma on the island since the first English settlers arrived has been attracting – and keeping – physicians. Compensation for a doctor on such a small island is not competitive with a mainland practice, and then there's the whole matter of finding someone willing to drop themselves into an insular community on a plot of land in the middle of the Chesapeake Bay. Making the right match always has been difficult, and even when someone is found it hasn't always worked out for the best.

Such as the "physician" in 1969 who seemed to be the answer to the island's prayers until a few days into his practice when he was summoned to deliver a baby, and a midwife who witnessed his work said it was obvious he didn't know what he was doing. When asked to produce his medical license, the man disappeared. He later was arrested on the mainland on drug charges and determined to be a fraud: he wasn't a doctor at all. But at least he didn't kill anybody, as Dr. J.D. Pitts did in 1884 when he drew a revolver and shot dead the island's other physician, Dr. L.T. Walter, abruptly ending a brief period when Tangier had two doctors. News reports at the time said Pitts had grown jealous of Walter's successful practice. Newman Thomas, who has researched the history of physicians on the island, said Pitts and Walter were in their 20s, fresh from the University of Maryland School of Medicine where they graduated a year apart. Pitts apparently had become addicted to morphine, and while he was away from the island having his addiction treated, Walter came over from the Eastern Shore to provide medical care. Pitts returned, apparently viewed Walter's involvement as stealing his patients and confronted Walters. A meeting at Pitts' office turned deadly.

Newman Thomas was born and raised in Deltaville, on Virginia's mainland, just across the bay from Tangier, which was home to one of his grandfathers. Thomas visited Tangier a few times as a kid, but didn't really grow interested in the island until a few years ago when he started putting together a family history. One thing led to another, and Thomas began spending a lot of time in libraries, poring over old newspapers and other documents and piecing together the island's past, including Tangier's struggle to bring in medical doctors. A by-product of his research was the answer to something he'd always wondered: the origin of his first name, Newman, which he shared with his grandfather. He discovered that

Newman was the surname of the physician who followed Pitts and Walter. Dr. James Frank Newman remained on Tangier for more than 16 years, Thomas said, and became the first resident physician to stay for any length of time.

"Everybody liked to name their kid after either the doctor or the preacher on the island," Thomas said. "My grandfather was named after him."

Newman, like Pitts and Walter, graduated from the University of Maryland School of Medicine in Baltimore, and for a time there seemed to be a pipeline between the school and the island. Following Newman from the university were Dr. Norman Ellis Sartorius and Dr. James Knox Insley. Dr. Willard Orville Daisy also arrived from Baltimore, but from a homeopathic college. Dr. Grover Bache Gill, a graduate of the Medical College of Virginia in Richmond, left Tangier when called into military service during World War I. None stayed for more than a few years. That all changed with Gill's replacement, Dr. Charles Frederick Gladstone, also a University of Maryland School of Medicine graduate, who moved to Tangier in 1918 and, remarkably, stayed for almost 40 years.

"Gladstone was a rock," said Thomas. "He was almost an idol."

In his research, Thomas found one of Gladstone's business cards, the front of which featured a drawing of a naked baby. But that didn't tickle Thomas as much as the fact he had business cards at all in a place as small as Tangier. "I'm sure he must have ordered one box," Thomas said with a laugh, "and had to throw some away."

Gladstone established a pre-paid health insurance plan on Tangier, collecting monthly fees from the islanders to cover any medical services they required. At one point, the fees were $1 for couples, $1.25 for couples with one child, $1.50 for two children, $1.75 for three and $2 for larger families, according to an interview Gladstone conducted with The Virginian-Pilot newspaper in Norfolk in February 1965. According to a historical marker on the island, Gladstone went door-to-door collecting the monthly fees and if the prescribed amounts were too steep for families he would accept whatever they could afford.

In The Virginian-Pilot column by Jim Mays, headlined "This Man Was Almost An Island," Gladstone was said to have truly become one of the islanders, having lived there for four decades. He treated their illnesses, bandaged their wounds, played poker with them in slow times and walked everywhere he went. At one point, he turned down an offer of a bicycle from the town council, according to the article in The Virginian-Pilot.

"When I get too old to walk," he said, "I'll retire!"

And over the course of 40 years, he helped birth a lot of babies on the island. According to one estimate, Gladstone delivered 2,000 babies during his time on the island, but no one knows for sure. Gladstone, who disposed of his records when he retired, lost count.

Gladstone announced he would indeed retire in 1954, and, for his service to the island, he would be awarded a certificate of appreciation signed by President Dwight Eisenhower. But Gladstone stayed three more years – until he was 78 years old – because the island couldn't find a replacement. When he finally retired, he settled on the Eastern Shore and at age 83 did something he'd never done before: he married.

Before Gladstone departed, the residents of Tangier, with considerable help from the Virginia Methodist Conference and others, built a clinic directly across from Swain Memorial United Methodist Church and named it the Gladstone Memorial Health Center. Despite the new facility, which was completed in 1957, Tangier still had difficulty recruiting another doctor.

The Virginia Council on Health and Medical Care recognized the island's dilemma and took up Tangier's cause, spearheading a national search for Gladstone's successor, but even its wide reach couldn't simplify the process. There was the Ukranian-born physician who considered moving to Tangier but couldn't pass the state boards. In a letter describing its involvement, the council noted a "lady physician" who expressed interest but was obligated to remain in the U.S. Army and did not want anyone to "spring" her from military service. The council wrote to soon-to-be-retiring military physicians, but found no luck there either.

Word of a Japanese-born doctor who might be a candidate came from a Chicago placement firm, but the problem was Dr. Mikio Kato had returned to Japan to care for his ailing father, and helping him navigate visa issues to get back into the United States appeared problematic. This was, after all, just more than a decade after the end of World War II. Kato was contacted, and the council persuaded him to take the Tangier job for at least a year and eventually helped him gain re-entry into the United States after Virginia Sen. Harry F. Byrd Sr. took the island's case to the Immigration and Naturalization Service.

When Kato arrived at the Baltimore airport in April 1957, he was greeted by reporters and photographers, and news of his arrival was published in newspapers around the country, including The New York Times, which had become intrigued by the island's public search for a physician. As the boat carrying Kato steamed into Tangier's harbor after dark, the sexton at Swain Memorial rang the church bell and residents swarmed the dock to greet their new physician.

That fall, Kato married his secretary, Emma Sue Crockett, a Tangier native, and a year later, lured by the clear promise of a more lucrative medical career on the mainland, the couple left Tangier so he could set up an obstetrics and gynecological practice in Maryland. Kato fulfilled his one-year contract (plus some) to Tangier, but the island was left once again without a resident physician.

In the late 1950s, an Eastern Shore physician, Dr. Isaac "Ike" White, began bringing his private boat, Island Doctor, to Tangier once a week as a stopgap measure. In 1961, a North Carolina physician, Dr. John E. Parks, moved to Tangier and took the job, and all went well until he was stricken with cancer. Parks had to leave the island from time to time for treatment, and he finally departed in late 1964 to never return.

In January 1965, the Huntley-Brinkley Report, the NBC television network's nightly news, produced a lengthy report on Tangier's physician-less plight, and other news outlets also aired and published pieces on the island. The Richmond Amateur Radio Club put out a call for help among ham radio operators around the world. As a result, more than 80 physicians contacted island officials. One of those doctors was Dr. Oscar M. Watson Jr., a Colorado physician who had a heart condition and was looking for something less strenuous than a full-time practice. Watson visited the island and accepted the job, news that was so welcome that a press conference was held at the state capitol in Richmond. Islanders built a home for its new physician, but Watson struggled with his health and died in 1969.

Then came the curious Edward T. Wiga, who posed as Dr. Joseph Wiga, a Hungarian who said he received his medical training in Leningrad. In actuality, he had only an 8th-grade education, but the islanders didn't learn that until he disappeared after his credentials were questioned by the midwife who noted he had no clue about birthing babies. He'd been on the job little more than a week. He later was arrested for possession of narcotics, according to news reports at the time.

Without a permanent physician, Tangier found itself in particular need in 1969 when five islanders contracted tuberculosis. The island's leadership summoned nurse-midwife Landon, the Tangier-born former medical missionary in Pakistan, and, according to her 2012 obituary, asked if she would come back and supervise the state of Virginia's program to eradicate tuberculosis on the island. She answered the call and wound up caring for Tangier's residents for several years as the island's primary medical caregiver.

"Doctor Jane," as she was known, tended to the residents' most rudimentary medical needs. In an emergency, she could even pull teeth. However, she accomplished much more as an advocate for healthy lifestyles, a noteworthy approach on an island dealing with issues such as chronic obesity and even tuberculosis, which was still a problem on Tangier in the 1960s. According to a 1974 article in People Magazine – titled "The Midwife on Tangier Island" – tuberculosis on the island vanished, and she launched a successful weight-loss clinic, though not everyone appreciated her zeal for healthy living. An unidentified islander complained in the People article that Landon "don't seem to pay you no mind unless you've flossed your teeth and lost a pound or two."

In 1979, David Nichols arrived. Would his time on Tangier be fleeting or would he stay? The people of Tangier were about to find out.

Bicycles are a primary mode of transportation on Tangier Island.
Bill Lohmann

Nichols and nurse Jenny Lasley prepare for takeoff to Tangier in 1980.
Beverly Orndorff/Richmond Times-Dispatch

FOUR

THE MISSION BEGINS

'I think for him this was his mission from God'

Nichols was awarded his pilot's license on Nov. 8, 1979, and he took Dianne flying that day in his newly acquired Cessna Skyhawk II. Precisely a week later, Nov. 15, a Thursday, he made his inaugural medical flight from Hummel Field in Topping, just across the Rappahannock River from White Stone. *To Tangier Is,* his pilot logbook reads, *to medical clinic for patient care w/ nurse + Dianne.* Jenny Lasley was the nurse.

Decades later, Nichols remembered little about that day other than it was a cold, windswept morning when he arrived on the island. Dianne Nichols recalled how the clinic, which she found small and underwhelming, was poorly equipped, which is why every week Nichols carried his medical supplies in fishing tackle boxes, hauling them back and forth from the plane to the clinic on each visit.

"We saw a lot of patients," Dianne recalled, but she made the trip to Tangier as David's nurse only twice. She was pregnant with Davy and had to arrange a sitter for Sarah, so it quickly became apparent it was just too complicated for her to travel regularly to Tangier, not knowing exactly when their work would be done and when they would arrive home from the island. There also was the matter of Nichols entering into what Dianne diplomatically described as "doctor mode" when he was on duty. Nichols laughed at the description and put it more bluntly: "She couldn't work with me. I'm too hard." In time, others would discover this side of him.

In those early years, Nichols felt it particularly important to travel to Tangier every Thursday when the weather permitted – and sometimes even when it didn't – to demonstrate his commitment. An article in the Eastern Shore News in March 1980 marveled that Nichols had been traveling to the island for four months and hadn't missed a week. Bad weather forced him to cancel one Thursday trip, but he made up for it by flying there the following Saturday and opening the clinic. Years later, Nichols described Dianne as "a saint" for accepting his devotion to Tangier, which was accompanied by long, unpredictable hours, and of course, the inherent danger of stepping into a plane to go to work. "It was a big sacrifice on her part, but she was always supportive," he said.

At the beginning, patients didn't make appointments to see Nichols; they just showed up and waited.

Sometimes there were few patients or none at all, though that didn't deter Nichols.

"Especially in the winter, sometimes we'd see nobody, but we always had our hot chocolate," said Rhonda Lawrence, one of the first nurses to join Nichols' practice. She noted that the hot chocolate was a source of warmth considering the clinic's balky furnace, and one of Nichols' last questions before leaving the mainland on winter mornings was, "Did you pack the hot chocolate?"

. "Regardless of whether we had three patients or five patients or no patients, he was determined to be there," she said. "Sometimes we just sat outside on the steps and talked and drank our hot chocolate."

Nichols started out making the 15-minute flight in a single-engine plane on his day off, an opportunity to combine doing good *and* flying, his new favorite pastime. As years peeled away, the island became part of his mainland practice, with other members of his practice traveling regularly to Tangier, and he graduated to piloting a helicopter on the weekly visits. In later years, the license plate on his car read: *DR COPTR*.

With a small staff, everyone in Nichols' White Stone practice wound up going to Tangier on occasion, and whenever Nichols interviewed someone for a position he made a point of telling them about this unique island – maybe even flying them over for a look. He talked about the wonderful, genuine people and their interesting way of speaking, which might be a little challenging to understand at first but how they would eventually catch on though they really didn't have a choice: the weekly visits were very much included in the job description. "This is part of your job, and if you don't like that, then don't come," he recalled telling them. "They always came."

Even if they arrived with trepidation.

"'How are you flying in small planes?'" Lawrence recalled Nichols asking her. "Well, I hadn't really done a lot of flying in small planes. I didn't always have a great time flying, but I never got sick."

Before each trip, the nurses packed the supplies and medicine in the tackle boxes – there was no pharmacy on the island – and stashed the patient charts and X-rays in canvas bags. They made a point of properly storing the super-cold liquid nitrogen (used to freeze warts and remove skin tags) in an insulated vacuum flask. As long as the simple but important instructions were followed – leave the lid a little loose for venting, and don't let the container tip over – nothing would blow up. Besides all of that, Lawrence and the others who regularly flew with Nichols also received basic lessons in the operation of a small plane. Not just the location of the cord that would release the emergency life raft, but how to check the fuel for water contamination and how to tie down the plane after landing on Tangier, among other things.

Beth Somers, who came to work for the practice after Lawrence and would make many trips to Tangier, remembered that Nichols even taught her how to land the plane.

"He said, 'Something could happen to me, and you need to know what to do,'" Somers recalled.

Sometimes in those early days, Nichols and who-ever was with him would secure the plane, unload it and then walk from the airfield to the clinic, a distance of no more than a half-mile – a nice stroll if you weren't lugging tackle boxes full of medical supplies and other gear. Eventually, arrangements were made for a golf cart to fetch the medical team and their belongings, which worked well except for the time the cart apparently hit a rather large bump or a pothole and Nichols got dumped on the road ("I heard laughter before I hit the ground," Nichols recalled years later, laughing himself, "just reams of laughter"). There also was the period when a construction project blocked the route, Lawrence recalled, and she and Nichols had to scale a fence and traipse through deep mud to reach the clinic.

"I couldn't hop the fence, so he'd have to get over it, and I'd hand him the equipment and our bags, and then he'd help me over the fence," said Lawrence, who laughed and acknowledged thinking more than once: "Is it worth all this?"

It definitely was, she determined, to Nichols.

One day it was so foggy that Lawrence didn't see how they could fly to Tangier, but they went to Hummel Field and gave it a shot. "Sometimes it opens up around the island," Nichols told her, "and we can land."

"I'm thinking, please God, get me through this," recalled Lawrence, a young mother at the time. "I had this little boy at home."

They flew across the bay above the fog, but couldn't see the island, so they returned to Topping. They waited an hour and tried again. Nothing doing. Nichols finally – and reluctantly – gave up.

"A rare day he did not get there," Lawrence said.

Sometimes when flying wasn't an option because of the weather, Nichols would arrange for a boat to carry him and anyone else from his staff to Tangier. "That's not when you'd want to be on the bay," said Rob Duffer with a laugh. Duffer is a physician assistant who worked with Nichols for almost two decades and regularly made the trip to Tangier. On one boat ride in rough seas, Duffer recalls 7-foot waves that jostled the passengers.

"As we got close to Tangier," Duffer recalled, "David says, 'Think about this: these are the types of trips people will talk about. They're not going to talk about trips that were nice and calm.'"

Nichols was determined and "compulsive," by his own estimation, to fulfill his commitment to the people of Tangier every week, but his reasoning was simple: "They are my patients, and I'm going to take care of them," he told his brother Scott on several occasions. Yet, Nichols was an exceedingly careful pilot, unwilling to take foolish chances or put anyone at risk. As a result, Somers recalled no close calls in all of her years of flying with Nichols, although there was the time a tire blew out as they tried to land at Hummel. Everything worked out fine, and they landed safely after Nichols made another pass at the airfield, but Somers joked years later that she "almost needed a tranquilizer" by the time she got home that night.

Years later, Lawrence marveled at Nichols' dedication when it came to Tangier, even in those early days when he barely knew the island. At the beginning, she wondered about his motivation for expending such effort, but not for long.

"Early on, I would have said it was for financial gain or ... he wanted a plane, a toy," she said. "Maybe at one point he did, but that quickly changed. I think his whole life became Tangier and his mission. I think his love for those people was just astounding, and their love for him. I think for him this was his mission from God."

While getting to the island Thursday mornings was one thing, leaving it Thursday evenings was sometimes quite another. Nichols and his staff experienced many late nights, arriving back at Hummel after dark, as a result of staying on the island longer than expected. "We'd hear the plane," said Tangier native Dewey Crockett, "and Mom would say, 'There's Dr. Nichols just leaving. Oh, I hope he gets home safe.'"

Many times, Nichols was late leaving because a patient walked in the clinic door at the last minute needing help, and Nichols wasn't about to leave and make them wait another week for medical care. Once in a while Nichols was already in his plane, packed up and ready to fly home, when someone would flag him down and tell him about an islander who was sick. Nichols would shut off the plane's engine and head back to the clinic.

"That was always hard," Nichols said. "But you would never leave a patient. Couldn't do that."

Some days, by the time the clinic was empty and Nichols and his nurses were finally ready to go, the weather – which can change quickly and dramatically in the bay – made it impossible for them to fly into tiny Hummel Field. Nichols would have to change plans and head for the larger airport in Newport News, where he kept an old car for just such occasions, and made the hour's drive home to White Stone, or sometimes a Tangierman would return them across the bay to White Stone by boat.

On rare occasions when the weather grew too perilous for flying at all, they were stranded on the island for the night. The first time that happened – in December 1979, less than a month after beginning his Tangier work – Nichols was still something of a stranger to the islanders, so no one discovered until later that he spent the night, without any food, sleeping on an examining room table in the clinic.

"When they found out I had stayed alone they were absolutely horrified," Nichols said many years later. "That never happened again. They always had space for me."

When they couldn't leave the island, Nichols and his nurses were invited into homes to stay the night, which presented complications for people like Somers who had young children and had to scramble to make arrangements for their care. At least Nichols and his staff had comfortable places to stay. They would arise early the next morning, fly back to the mainland, head home to get a shower and then return to the White Stone office for a full day of seeing patients there.

In the years before Nichols arrived on the island, health care on Tangier was in transition. The island's dif-

ficulty in attracting physicians and then convincing them
to stay made access to medical care restrictive at worst
and inconvenient at best for the people of Tangier. Nichols would say years later the residents of Tangier hadn't
been underserved medically, they had been *unserved*,
which was not entirely correct as physicians and den-
tists periodically visited the island. But there is no doubt
the people who lived on the island were not the primary
focus of healthcare practitioners. The overall unpredict-
ability of hometown medical care left many on Tangier to
seek medical care in Maryland – which was accessible by
year-round ferry service – or not at all. Visiting a doctor
in Maryland – including the ferry ride to Crisfield and
the cab fare to the physician's office – was not an inex-
pensive proposition in money and time. Such visits could
prove to be all-day events, and many Tangiermen, particularly older ones, just didn't bother.

"What was happening was most of the people
just weren't going to the doctor," said Cindy Parks, who
many years later went to work for Nichols in the clinic's
office. "My grandmother, as she got older, refused to go
to the doctor … and we have a lot of people like that. I
know my grandmother lived five years longer than she
would have just because Dr. Nichols was here."

Yet, at first, Nichols had to overcome the islanders' suspicions and skepticism. Who is this new doctor?
Why is he here? How long before he leaves? Some, who
might have recalled the days of Charles Gladstone and

his flat fee of no more than $2 per family per month, thought Nichols charged too much. They knew he operated a successful practice on the mainland, which led to the inevitable conclusion that he was merely one of those modern, business-first physicians who viewed the island as an additional source of revenue. Tangierman can be a little stubborn – as Tangiermen acknowledge – when it comes to accepting a new way of doing things or a new face doing them.

"It doesn't come easy," said Dewey Crockett, who grew up on Tangier, left the island to work as a United Methodist minister for a few years and then returned home, becoming deeply involved in the community, including a stint as mayor. "You have to really prove yourself for them to accept you. When he first came here, there was always the critical bunches [saying], 'Well, he's just here to make money.' Then when he started coming every Thursday, even in stormy weather, [they were saying], 'Well, he wants that extra money.' Then they saw how faithful he was, and the money thing dropped, [and they said], 'This man's got a love for us to come the way he comes.' That broke the ice. I'd say after the first four or five years, they accepted him wholeheartedly. I'm just amazed how much he fell in love with Tangier, and the people of Tangier fell in love with him, too."

As Crockett spoke in late 2010, he was lying in bed, the covers pulled up to his neck. His health had been

in decline for years: kidney disease, a broken hip and car-
diac arrest followed by heart bypass surgery. Nichols was
by his side through it all.

"Oh, my, I'd been dead a long time ago if it hadn't
been for him," Crockett said. "I've had multiple problems, and he stayed on top of all of them. Sent me where
I needed to go when he felt like he'd exhausted everything he could do. He's more than just a doctor to me."

A long and abiding interest in medical matters led
Crockett to become a close friend of Nichols. As a teenager, Crockett had volunteered at the clinic when Watson
was the island's physician. As his interest grew, so did his
involvement. Watson sent him to hospitals in Richmond
to learn about laboratory work and X-rays so that he
could help during the summers when he was home from
college. As a student, Crockett assisted Watson in the
delivery of more than 20 babies on the island.

"Dr. Watson always wanted me to go to medical
school," Crockett said. "Only thing that kept me out of
medical school is I didn't think I could afford it, but I
always had a hunger for medical things."

Crockett left Tangier to attend college and semi-
nary and then served as a church pastor on the Eastern
Shore of Virginia and Maryland. By the time he and his
wife, Jean, felt the tug of home and returned in 1984,
Nichols had become a fixture on the island. Over the

years, the Crocketts threw themselves into the life of Tangier. They helped start an ambulance service to replace the island's previous means of transporting medical patients, which was actually a stretcher stashed in the back of a pickup truck.

As a nurse, Jean had worked closely with Nichols before becoming an English teacher at the Tangier school. Jean didn't grow up on her Tangier, but her mother did and she visited often as a child and loved the place. Jean said she used to worry that she would marry someone who wouldn't want to come to Tangier. She solved that by marrying Dewey Crockett. She would work with Nichols on Thursdays, and she became his eyes and ears and stethoscope the other six days of the week, following up with patients, taking on new cases that didn't require a physician and handling tasks for the mainland public health department. She also served as liaison for Eastern Shore Rural Health System, a public health agency that sent a revolving cast of medical personnel to the island on a regular basis for a number of years until the island's clinic no longer met accreditation requirements, which put a stop to the public funding that enabled the visits. For Crockett, there was an undeniable pressure that went with being the only full-time health care provider living on the island.

"You were never off-call," she said. "But I knew it was going to be that way. I've had a tremendous love for this island, and I was thrilled to be able to live here. I felt called to be a missionary … and this was my mission. I'm right where I want to be. This is my place."

Jean Crockett said she had done all kinds of nursing in all kinds of settings, but she had never encountered anyone like Nichols.

"He was one of the best doctors I ever worked with," she said. "There are few David Nichols around."

Having seen him up close, she didn't buy the cynicism of some on the island that Nichols merely came to the island as a way to line his pockets. She knew he was losing money on the Tangier part of his practice. She also knew he loved having a weekly excuse to fly, but she is convinced that is not what kept him coming to Tangier, week after week.

"He got a lot more out of it than he thought he was going to get out of it," she said.

As for Dewey, he taught social studies at the school and served as the island's undertaker, a job he started performing as a teen. He was only 10 or 12 when he started helping the gravedigger and placing flowers at the church and making other arrangements for funerals. He worked his way up to assisting the mainland undertaker who would come to Tangier whenever anyone died. It wasn't the sort of work most boys would aspire to, but on a small island you tend to look for ways to be of service to your neighbors, and you never know what might grab you as interesting and make you feel needed.

During summers, after returning to the island, Dewey returned to his roots: volunteering in the Tangier clinic. He worked as a medical technician, taking blood-pressure readings, drawing blood and assisting Nichols any way he could.

"He was a good teacher," Crockett said of Nichols. "He'd say, 'Have you ever done this before?' I'd say, 'No, sir,' and then he'd show me and say, 'Now, next time, I expect *you* to do it.'"

Crockett laughed, not because what he said was so funny, but because what he said was a shared truth – part inside joke, part badge of honor – for anyone who worked for Nichols, who was indeed a good teacher and who did indeed harbor high expectations of his students.

"Once he showed you something, he expected you to remember it," Crockett said. "He would keep after all of us who worked for him. It was the School of Hard Knocks."

And David Nichols was the headmaster.

When the weather is warm, local children enjoy diving from docks into Tangier harbor after the ferries depart in the afternoon, as 12-year-old Nathan Crockett does here in May 2007. *Bob Brown/Richmond Times-Dispatch.*

FIVE

Splendid Isolation
'I find no place like this island'

In 1608, a year after a group of English settlers changed the course of North American history by establishing a colony at Jamestown, Captain John Smith left the relative comfort of that palisade fort and set off on another voyage of discovery. With a crew of 14, Smith sailed a shallop toward the mouth of the James River and into open water, embarking on an exploration of the Chesapeake Bay and its tributaries.

Over the course of that summer, he encountered Native Americans, all manner of wildlife and one adventure after another, but in his pursuit of the region's natural riches, he found no gold or silver. He and his crew, however, come upon numerous small, uninhabited islands in the bay, including the one that would become known as Tangier. In his journal, he referred to the collection of islands as Russell's Isles, named in honor of the physician who was along for the trip. The map he produced from the expedition – the first map of Virginia that was so accurate and reliable subsequent explorers used it for decades to come – made note of the cluster of islands, including Tangier.

Smith and his crew, of course, weren't the first humans to see Tangier. The Pocomoke Indians are said to have used the island for hunting and fishing long before the English arrived and began settling there. An often-told story that seems to be more myth than fact is that a John Crockett arrived with his family in the late 1600s, but the first evidence of English residents on the island is 1778 when Joseph Crockett purchased 475 acres of Tangier. Time too has clouded when and why Tangier became known as Tangier (and who bestowed the name). Some believe there is a distant connection to the Moroccan city of the same name and that perhaps John Smith himself, who had visited the other Tangier, had labeled the island. Others are not so sure. Regardless of the origin, "Tangier," in references to the island, began showing up on maps and legal records in the late 1600s. By 1800, the island's population was 79.

In the early days of white settlement on Tangier, farming was the primary occupation and cattle the chief moneymaker, as the island functioned as a naturally unfenced pasture for livestock. Fishing didn't become the favored means of making a living – and a way of life – until later in the 1800s when modern transportation made it a more feasible occupation with the arrival of the railroad to the Eastern Shore and the development of the steamboat line throughout the bay, which opened a gateway to the markets of the Northeast for Tangiermen and others harvesting oysters, and later crabs. The 1930s invention of the crab pot – a wire cage-like contraption for trapping crabs – helped the crab industry really take off, wrote David L. Shores, author of "Tangier Island: Place, People and Talk," a well-researched book about the island published in 2000. Before that, wrote Shores, professor emeritus of English at Old Dominion University who was born on Tangier and grew up on the mainland, crabbing was largely "a casual and leisure-time activity." The seafood business fueled a rise in population on Tangier, which topped 1,000 in 1900 and reached its peak of more than 1,100 by 1930, though it has been dropping precipitously ever since.

In the early 1800s, religion gained a foothold on Tangier's shores when Joshua Thomas, a boatman-turned-Methodist preacher who became known as "the parson of the islands," began holding camp meetings on the beach that attracted followers from around the bay. At around the same time, the British military gained its own foothold on Tangier, taking over the island for tactical reasons and constructing a fort. At one point, 12,000 troops were stationed on Tangier, giving the British a convenient launching pad for assaults on Washington and

Baltimore during the war of 1812. The way the story is told, the British commanding officer asked Thomas to preach a sermon for the soldiers before they attacked Baltimore in September 1814. Thomas preached, but he did not say what the British leadership had in mind. In his sermon, Thomas declared the mission evil and warned the British of an impending defeat, saying God had revealed to him that they would lose the battle. They did, and the battle proved to be a major turning point in the war and also inspired Francis Scott Key to compose "The Star-Spangled Banner." Three months later the Treaty of Ghent was signed, ending the war. (The British fort was situated on a part of Tangier that long ago washed away, and whatever might be left of the fort is beneath the bay.)

The anti-British preaching of Pastor Thomas was but one example of the islanders' deep-rooted religious faith, which has manifested itself over the years in old-time revival meetings and more municipal matters such as declining to sell alcohol (bring your own, but be discreet), and in recent years, painting a Christian cross on the island's water tower (with a crab on the other side).

Tangiermen have long bowed to the authority of a higher power. In his book, Shores told the story of a great storm in 1821 that swept flood waters over much of the island, an event the most religious viewed "as a providential sign and intrusion in their lives to encourage greater devotion among those who 'believed' and a warning to the unbelievers to get 'right with their Lord.'" In his "A Brief History of Tangier Island, Va.," published about 1900, the Rev. C.P. Swain, minister of the island's Methodist church which later was named for him, marveled that the "writer has not heard the name of the Deity taken profanely by an inhabitant of the place in two years, though as pastor his duties call him into every nook and corner at almost all times of the night and day." He also proudly related that "a liquor saloon has never been able to exist, even though … such an evil is lawful."

That devotion to faith has, in some ways, defined them as a people and led to bold stands through history while also leaving them, at times, out-of-step with those from away and occasionally in conflict with one another.

During the Civil War, Tangier felt the tug of its allegiances to state, neighbor and church. The island was, of course, part of Virginia, home of Richmond, the capital of the Confederacy, but nearby Maryland remained in the Union. However, religion held the greatest pull. The Tangier church was affiliated with the Northern Methodist Church, which opposed slavery, so the islanders followed their denomination's lead and declined to join the rest of Virginia and the Confederacy, leading to an alienation from much of the rest of its home state, according to Shores' research. As Swain wrote, "Be it said, however, to the credit of this people, that a Secession banner never waved over it; it never would consent to go out of the Union … I have been told that a slave was never held by anybody living on it."

Alcohol has never been sold on the island, and on occasion authorities have gone to great lengths to keep it that way. In July 1937, Mayor W.T. Crockett, his son and the Rev. J.C. Bolton boarded a boat to investigate a report that alcohol was being sold. In an ensuing scuffle, the mayor and his son were tossed overboard, and the mayor also was stabbed with a boathook. However, according to a report by an Accomack County deputy sheriff, reported in the Danville Bee newspaper, "The preacher was too quick for them." Three men were arrested. They acknowledged to the deputy sheriff that they had about a pint of liquor with them, but they insisted they weren't selling it. The mayor survived.

For a long time, the church minister often acted as arbiter in disputes on the island, rendering outside law enforcement unnecessary, according to an Associated Press report in 1933. Nonetheless, Accomack County, of which Tangier is a part, thought it was being helpful by shipping a ready-to-assemble jail to the island. According to the AP story, Tangier residents took that as an affront to their honor and "tossed it into the sea."

In the 1940s, Tangier's only church, by then known as Swain Memorial, went through an ugly split over doctrinal differences. The church's pastor and some congregants left and established another church, New

Testament, which eventually settled just down the road from Swain. There were reports, according to Shores' book, of a sinking of the minister's boat (twice), vandalism (including an organ used for church services thrown in a ditch) and otherwise general ugliness between the quarreling parties, which of course, becomes amplified in such a small, insulated place.

There were similar hard feelings five decades later when the island turned down the allure of Hollywood money based on its conservative Christian values. In 1996, Warner Bros. wanted to film scenes on the island for a movie called "Message in a Bottle," starring Paul Newman and Kevin Costner. However, the town council read the script beforehand, objected to the language, sex and alcohol in the story and voted unanimously against allowing the movie to be made on the island. Not everyone on the island felt that way. The issue proved contentious as strenuous arguments were made by islanders (and those off the island whose livelihoods were tied to tourism on Tangier) hoping to cash in on having so many visitors during the filming and after the film hit theaters. In the end, not even a visit from Newman himself – he wore a cap and dark glasses and didn't have much to say other than reportedly declaring the island one of the most beautiful places he'd ever visited – could sway the council. The vote stood, and the cast and crew wound up filming in Maine.

Tangier's mayor at the time, Dewey Crockett, was quoted by *The Baltimore Sun* as acknowledging the film was "a once-in-a-lifetime opportunity for our little island. It would have increased revenue and tourism, but there are more important things than money, aren't there?"

Faith has fueled its resilience through difficult times. Islanders have weathered the worst of Mother Nature – hot and cold. There's no more precarious spot than a tiny, low-lying island with an approaching hurricane churning the seas. Though some islanders flee to the mainland when such action is recommended by authorities in the face of an approaching storm, many Tangiermen choose to stay put and not abandon their homes, a reflection of their firm belief they will be looked after by a higher power, as well as their bravery and their stubbornness.

Tangier has survived its share of summer storms sloshing bay water over the island, flooding homes and destroying oyster beds – the hurricane of August 1933 was a particularly brutal storm – but winter can unleash its own particular brand of harshness. Relentlessly long periods of freezing temperatures have left the island icebound, occasionally for more than a few days at a time, as in 1936 when the deep freeze shut off Tangier from the outside world – at least by boat – for more than two months. Islanders who have survived such episodes tell stories of walking on the frozen bay a considerable distance from shore, even to the mainland itself, for provisions. One time, a blimp was called in to deliver food. Tangier was ice-bound most recently in January 2018.

"When I was a kid, we used to get our sleighs and go out on the ice just about every winter," said Burke Landon, who grew up on Tangier in the 1940s and never left. "There are these old ships a couple of miles out in the bay, target ships [for military practice], and people walked right out to them."

Landon and his wife, Bonnie, also a Tangier native, said they never lived anywhere else and couldn't imagine wanting to.

"My Lord, no," said Burke, who worked more than a half-century as a waterman and was still at it at the time of a 2010 interview at age 75. "This is somewhere you can let your children go out and run all over the island and not worry about them. I've been from Florida to Boston, but I find no place like this island."

Said Tangier native Norma Dize, "The only time I wanted to move away was when a hurricane was coming! Then I'd go away for a while." But she always came back.

The splendid isolation of Tangier is both its charm and its curse, and those who love the island and entertain no desire to ever leave – even during hurricanes when they must endure howling winds and flood waters lapping at their front stoops – believe it has always been more splendid than isolated. Calling the island community "close-knit" or like "one big family" is almost an understatement; the majority of Tangier natives have the surnames of Parks, Pruitt or Crockett.

"There's not a soul on here that I don't know their names," said Dize, who added with a laugh, "Sometimes you know too much about them, or they might know too much about you."

There is no doubt that living in a land apart has enabled their manner of speaking to survive in an increasingly homogeneous world. Through the years, the generally accepted explanation is that their dialect, intonation and vocabulary derive from the islanders' British ancestors or is representative of some form of "Elizabethan English." Not so, wrote Shores, the retired English professor and author of "Tangier Island: Place, People and Talk." He believes the way the islanders speak is simply just another dialect of American English that has evolved over time. The islanders' ancestors did indeed come primarily from Britain, but from all parts and at different times, so it's impossible to point to one place or period as the source of Tangier's dialect.

Similar to other small, isolated coastal communities along the Atlantic seaboard, Tangier has maintained a distinctive manner of speaking for generations, different from residents of the nearby mainland. Words such as "high" are pronounced "h-ah-ee" and "crib" becomes "cr-ih-uh-b," Shores wrote.

Vocabulary also takes some getting used to for non-Tangiermen. Examples from "Tangier Talk," a publication authored by lifelong resident Bruce Gordy, include "He's in a kelter!" which is Tangierese for "He's very upset!" and "She can talk the flood down!" means "She never stops talking!" When asked for a few examples, Inez Pruitt said other island sayings include "Were i' ye?" (Where are you?), "She's fair" (She is very good), "They just come for a mess a greens" (They came for a visit and stayed way too long), "He needs a bun" (He is talking too much), "I went mud larking today and found a bunch of diddles" (I was walking through the marshy and muddy areas and found a nest of baby ducks), "Well she's ugly" (She is very pretty), "He's hard to look at" (He is handsome).

It can require serious listening for visitors to understand a Tangierman, something Nichols discovered. He came to enjoy the local talk, and his favorite saying was "You ain't purdy none," which means "You're beautiful."

"There was always something with language that would catch us off guard occasionally," said Duffer, the physician assistant. "The (Tangier) staff protected us quite well. We'd have that look in our eyes, like deer in the headlights, and they would interpret for us."

One day a woman came in complaining of vision problems. What, Nichols asked, was she seeing? "Sut tags," it sounded like she said.

That one stopped him in his tracks.

"Wait a minute," Nichols said. "Say that again."

She did. "Sut tags."

Turns out, she was seeing "floaters" -- small specks in your field of vision that are actually shadows cast on your retina by tiny clumps of gel inside the vitreous of the eye, according to the American Academy of Ophthalmology.

What she was saying in her description is they reminded her of the small pieces of debris that float amid the smoke from a chimney, Pruitt said, something the patient considered "soot tags," which with her dialect came out "sut tag" to Nichols' ears.

The intrusion of the outside world through modern communications and ease of travel seems to have softened the Tangier dialect, particularly when islanders are speaking to visitors and tend to dial down their dialect out of courtesy – or self-consciousness. Shores believes some islanders are embarrassed by the way their speech is viewed by outsiders and make an effort to "talk proper" when in mixed company. That's a shame because the dialect is one of Tangier's endearing traits, an unmistakable part of the island culture and an opportunity for outsiders to broaden their own education and appreciation of others. It also might help to consider an alternate perspective, that no matter the place in question, those who are visiting are the only ones who talk funny.

Change always has come slowly to Tangier. This is a place that didn't get home telephone service until 1966 and produced its own electricity with three diesel-powered generators before underwater cables laid in the late 1970s brought power from the mainland. In 2010, the island was wired for high-speed Internet, leading to an unexpected burst of national exposure through a series of entertaining commercials for ESPN3.com (the sports network's online streaming service now known as ESPN3) that touted Tangier, tongue-in-cheek, as "the biggest sports town in America ... per capita." The Martin Agency, a Richmond-based advertising agency, chose Tangier to promote the online sports channel because here was a place where, despite its remoteness, residents could watch sporting events from around the world.

The spots featured, of course, the lovely island scenery and the distinctive dialect, but also the people of Tangier – 'It would be tragic to go there and have [professional] actors," said Andy Stockton, senior art director at Martin – showcasing their good nature and dry humor. For the cameras, they waved flags in support of the Georgia Bulldogs and UCLA Bruins and played tennis on the island airstrip. One resident atop the town's water tower unfurled a "Go Beavers" sign to cover one that read "Go Ducks" just to show the Oregon State-Oregon rivalry was alive and well 3,000 miles from the Pacific coast. Two Tangiermen, entranced by a cricket match on the screen, earnestly analyzed the delivery style of a bowler the way they might critique a baseball pitcher or a particularly graceful ballerina. Dorothea Pruitt, wearing an Alabama Crimson Tide shirt, stood before a white home accented with red shutters and declared, "Roll Tide!" (In another spot, she acknowledged having a crush on Alabama football coach Nick Saban.) Tangier Mayor James "Ooker" Eskidge held up a crab with its claws spread apart not unlike the hand signal made by Texas Longhorn fans and proclaimed, "Hook 'em, Horns!"

"It was the most fun shoot I've ever worked on," said Stockton, who had never visited the island before working on the commercials but had always wondered about it, having seen it for years far below on frequent flights over the bay between Richmond and New York. "Every time I go there, I love it more."

After the project, Stockton became a regular visitor to the island and in getting to know the island, he became familiar with Tangier's challenges and set to work making a documentary to showcase the island's plight.

In his 1900 history, Swain wrote: "The island is not more than five miles from tip to tip, north and south, nor much exceeding three-fourths of a mile in width at any place." It's a lot smaller now. Regardless, the island has never been an easily measured single strip of land but several irregularly shaped patches of largely tree-less ground separated by marshes and meandering tidal creeks that Tangiermen call "ditches." Homes are built along ridges that rise no more than a foot or three above sea level and are linked by glorified footbridges. At one time, Tangier consisted of a half-dozen such ridges, but long-term erosion and rising sea levels have washed away much of what used to be Tangier, and now only three ridges remain inhabited: Main Ridge, West Ridge and Canton. Nowadays, you can briskly walk the entire island in an hour, but years ago the population was ap-proximately double what it is now and each community was self-contained with its own shops and built-in neigh-borhood friends. Children grew up thinking the other side of the island might as well have been the other side of the world.

"When I was a child I never went to the other parts of the island, we only stayed up here in our vicinity playing with children here," said Virginia "Ginny" Mar-shall, who was born in 1927 and didn't meet her future husband, Smith, until they were teens, even though they were the same age, attended the same school and he lived in Canton, which is nothing more than a long stroll from her home on the Main Ridge. Marshall shrugged. That's just the way it was. Then they courted for three years.

"What the boys did back then was say, 'Can I walk with you?'" They wore a path around the island and then were married for 56 years until Smith's death in 2007. Children growing up on Tangier in the relentlessly connected 21st century with cable television and the Internet enjoy greater contact with the wider world than their parents and grandparents did, but they miss out on childhood in a less complicated time when outside distractions were fewer. If you were Ginny Marshall, excitement was going out on a small boat with her sister and catching crabs with a string, a nail and a chunk of fatback, or anticipating the arrival of the Sears Wish Book before Christmas.

"It was just different here then," Marshall said, sitting in the living room of her home, two doors down from the house where she grew up. "Just different."

Life was similar for Jean Autry, who grew up in the same era with Marshall and would fish and crab and do the sorts of things one would expect on an island. "A lot of people would come here and say, 'How can you live here with nothing to do?'" Autry said. "But we always found something to do. It's a beautiful, beautiful place to live."

Even a simple pastime such as softball gives a glimpse into how much Tangier has changed. Not that many decades ago, Tangier's population could field four or five teams – representing the various parts of the island – and the island had its own ball diamond, often hosting teams from nearby Smith Island. The ball field went away, however, when it was replaced in the late 1990s with a new school building. For several years, a team of Tangierman would charter a ferry and ride to nearby Smith Island to play on a lighted field there, but after a while, evening ballgames became too much for watermen on an early schedule.

"You'd get home at 10 or 11 o'clock at night and have to get up at 2:30," said Dan Dise, a Tangier waterman and one of the players. "It kept wearing on you."

By 2018, Tangier had several restaurants specializing, naturally, in seafood (although most are open only seasonally) and an ice cream parlor, Spanky's, which plays 1950s music and is pretty much the extent of commercial nightlife. Years back, when there were more forms of entertainment on the island, the building that houses Tangier's post office used to be a grocery store with a room in the back that served as a dance hall and movie theater. The island has a single grocery store, where Thursdays are big days: that's the day when the weekly shipment of food arrives from a Richmond wholesaler by way of a boat from Crisfield.

The speed limit on Tangier roads is 15 mph, which is generally not too difficult to obey since there are few vehicles on the island beyond golf carts, scooters and bicycles. It's not yet to the point that visitors come to Tangier to watch for Tangiermen driving golf carts – or to make note of the raised parking platforms that keep the carts above high-tide flooding – the way tourists flock to Pennsylvania Dutch Country in south central Pennsylvania to see the Amish horse-and-buggies, but their mode of transportation is viewed by some as an eccentric novelty.

A number of Tangier residents keep cars in Maryland, so they have transportation on the mainland when they travel there to shop, visit medical specialists or head off on vacation. (Yes, people who live on islands go elsewhere for vacation.) In fact, residents of Tangier, just six miles south of the Maryland state line, often feel more of a kinship with their Maryland neighbors than fellow Virginians, largely because the only daily, year-round ferry runs from Crisfield, about a dozen miles to the north, and Maryland provides the easiest-to-reach amenities of "city life" – such as shopping malls and hospitals.

"We have our ups and downs like any community has, but this is a close community," said Dewey Crockett, the former mayor and Tangier native, before his death in 2012. "It's peaceful and quiet here. Things are centered around school and church, and it's just a good community spirit. Very kind, loving people."

Crockett, the former mayor who lived away from the island for many years, felt the love and caring of his neighbors after returning home and experiencing a series of serious health problems. "When I was out of work we never went lacking," he said, lying in his bed at home, as he recuperated from a hospital stay during which he had a pacemaker implanted. "The community took care of us, finances and food and what have you. They were just here by our side. When somebody's hurting here, everybody's hurting. When somebody's happy, everybody's happy. It's just one big family."

Outsiders, however, haven't always felt that warmth. Tourism has long played a role in island life, but visitors sometimes have come away underwhelmed by the experience. Part of the reason could be a matter of misguided expectations: tourists might anticipate something very different than what they find on the island. A visit to Tangier is not a holiday at a Disney park; it's a stopover in someone else's real life, which can be a little awkward for all involved, particularly when those who live there can be, by their own admission, a little hard to get to know. In recent years, outsiders recognizing the true beauty of Tangier and wanting to help the island take advantage of what it has to offer led to the launching of a renewed emphasis on tourism. The campaign featured a number of nice, significant touches, including converting a former gift shop into a museum and visitors center.

Tangier is nothing if not authentic. The thin, fetching beach that curls around the southern tip of Tangier stands in pristine contrast to other features of the island: the working harbor, the trash incinerator and the airstrip, built in 1969 and just over 2,400 feet in length, which welcomes visitors flying in for lunch or on business and is the destination for nearby mainland pilots who deliver holly and Christmas toys every December as part of the annual Holly Run. The airfield also serves as the site of the island's homecoming party every August, a down-home, county fair-like atmosphere that brings many former residents back to the island for a weekend of sharing memories and rekindling friendships.

Tangier is not a resort; it's a small, quiet, old-fashioned town that has more than its share of challenges and rough edges. More than a few houses stand vacant and have fallen into disrepair from flooding or neglect, standing out sadly next to tidy homes with manicured lawns behind white picket fences. A fine, relatively new schoolhouse serves the island's children, the last remaining K-12 public school in Virginia under one roof and a natural community gathering spot, but enrollment has been heading south of 100 for years. Once students graduate, their options for employment on the island are so limited many leave to attend college, find a job or join the military. Fewer and fewer come back to live.

And the health of the islanders is an ongoing concern. In the 1800s, the island endured a series of epidemics – cholera, tuberculosis, measles and smallpox. The cholera epidemic in 1866 caused the island to be evacuated and residents did not return until the following year, according to the Accomack-Northampton Planning District Commision. In more recent times, there has been an inordinately high incidence of heart disease and pulmonary disorders on Tangier, caused or exacerbated by poor dietary habits, a lack of ready access to fresh fruit and vegetables, and cigarette smoking, all complicated perhaps by genetic factors in such a closely related community. Even now, barely a week goes by that a Tangierman isn't airlifted to a hospital – usually in Maryland, Salisbury or Baltimore, since the Maryland State Police typically provide the transportation – for emergency medical care, often due to heart attacks and the like.

The island even has its own sickness: Tangier Disease, a rare, inherited disorder characterized by enlarged, discolored tonsils and severely low levels of high density lipoprotein (often referred to as "good cholesterol") that can lead to an accumulation of cholesterol throughout the body and the development of premature arterial and cardiovascular disease. According to reports, the original case involved a Tangier boy having his tonsils removed in 1960. His tonsils were an odd orange color, and doctors – later including researchers from the National Institutes of Health – went looking to determine the cause. They found his sister had the same condition, and they determined they had inherited it from their parents, each of whom was a carrier of the guilty mutated gene but neither of whom exhibited symptoms similar to their children's.

According to the NIH's Genetics Home Reference on the National Library of Medicine's website for consumer information about genetic conditions, Tangier disease is a rare disorder with approximately 100 cases identified worldwide, though more cases are likely undiagnosed.

On top of everything else, the people of Tangier now are staring into a forbidding future when their island is no longer there.

Sunrise over Tangier harbor.
Bill Lohmann

SIX

ENDANGERED
*'They've still got some time, but
they're running out'*

On Tangier, the watermen arise hours ahead of the
sun. They dress, swallow cups of coffee and go to work
on their boats long before most people on the mainland
even consider crawling out of bed. Across the island, the
predawn darkness hums with the whine of golf carts and
the low murmur of distant conversations. Light streams
from the windows of the Double Six, a hole-in-the-wall
place that serves egg sandwiches and strong coffee and
keeps watermen's hours, meaning it seems to be open
only when it's dark. At the dock, the breeze slaps a rope
rhythmically against a flagpole, while an occasional boat
motors through the harbor. On this August morning, an
old-timer – a former waterman long past his working
days but still feeling the draw of the harbor in the early
morning – sits at a picnic table, his only companion a cup
of coffee, its steam swirling dreamily into the dimness

before daybreak. His presence and patience are rewarded soon enough: the sun, disguised as an orange ball of fire, climbs above the quiet harbor, the darkened crab houses and the bay beyond.

A few minutes later, James W. "Ooker" Eskridge Jr., pulled his 20-foot open workboat alongside the dock and as a greeting asks, "Did you see the sunrise?" His voice was filled with wonder and joy, hoping no one had missed the scene. "Not a bad job when you can watch the sunrise every morning."

Eskridge frequently experiences the brilliant dawns and always with clear-eyed appreciation. During the warm-weather crabbing season, he is generally up by 2 a.m. Not long after, he is toiling away in his crab shanty in the harbor – one of the numerous small shacks on stilts in the water – under the ghostly glow of bare bulbs strung over homemade shedding tanks, sorting and boxing so-called soft crabs to ship to market in New York.

James "Ooker" Eskridge, Tangier mayor and waterman, pulls in a crab pot on the Chesapeake Bay in August 2011.
Bill Lohmann

Eskridge fishes the soft crabs – blue crabs that have shed their external skeletons, or are about to – and sell for higher prices than hard crabs, though he catches hard crabs, too. For many, soft crabs are the most delectable way to consume crabs because they can be battered or dusted with flour, lightly fried and eaten whole. No peeling, no picking, no problem. At their most basic, fried soft crabs are served between slices of white bread – as they are at the dockside lunch counter at Tangier's harbor or just down the road at Lorraine's Seafood Restaurant – resulting in a sandwich that has the somewhat unnerving appearance of looking as if it has sprouted legs. Or they can be presented in upscale restaurants, attractively arranged in a more sophisticated manner on a platter. Either way, they're plenty good.

At first light, Eskridge delivers his boxes of soft crabs to the dark and quiet mailboat, tied at the main Tangier dock, more than an hour before it departs for the Maryland shore. After unloading, he points his boat toward open water in search of the bay's treasured blue crabs. He heads for a quiet, shallow inlet a few miles north of Tangier, Spain Cove, where he has staked out his crabbing ground. "There are two types of watermen," he said with a smile. "Watermen who look for crabs, and watermen who look for other watermen." Eskridge has done this sort of work so well for so long that he knows where to look for the crabs. He has placed more than 200 crab pots – in reality, they are ingenious, box-shape traps made of galvanized wire, heavy enough to sink to the bay bottom – laid out in long rows throughout the cove. He will work under the relentless summer sun until early afternoon, collecting the day's catch, hauling the pots from the bay floor and wrestling with the thick sea grasses that have tangled with the pots and lines.

"This is not a good job," he said as he worked, "if you don't enjoy it."

Commercial crabbing wasn't much of a job at all around the bay until advances in technology in the mid 19th century. Before that era, crabs were too perishable for anything more than local commerce, wrote William W. Warner in "Beautiful Swimmers," his 1976 book about the Atlantic blue crab and the Chesapeake Bay that won the Pulitzer Prize. However, the advent of regular steamship travel up and down the bay, the coming of the railroad to the Eastern Shore and the innovation of manufactured ice made the catching, transporting and preserving of crabs a practical enterprise. The development of the modern crab pot made it possible.

For Eskridge and others, this is how the process goes: he moves his boat alongside one of the floating markers tethered to a pot, and using a long hook, he snatches the rope secured to the pot, grabs the marker's neon yellow top, and then pulls the pot into the boat. He shakes out the crabs into a wooden tray in the boat's bow, picking out the ones that are, by law, too small to keep and throwing them back, tossing the keepers with speed and precision into baskets or containers of water, separating them depending on their size and whether they've shed their shells. He throws more back into the bay than he keeps. Then he drops an empty pot into the water and putters on to the next marker, a few yards away to repeat the routine, over and over again on row after row of pots.

Hypnotically monotonous, it is hard, solitary, back-bending work, but it's not over even when he returns to harbor in the afternoon. Then he must separate the crabs into the proper tanks at his crab house and check the shedding progress of the previously caught crabs, sort again since shedding is a natural, ongoing, time-sensitive and delicate process. Crabs grow by periodically molting – casting off their hard outer shell – and then forming a new shell. The process doesn't take long, so if you wait even a few hours too long and the new shell starts to form, you can no longer sell the crabs as soft crabs.

After his work is done at his crab house, Eskridge heads across the harbor to the fuel dock where he will gas up his boat and grab a couple of tall bags of ice that will keep the crabs fresh that he will box and send to market the following morning on the mail boat to Maryland. He arrives home by 4 p.m., but then needs to return to the crab shanty in early evening to check on the crabs and work a while longer. He often won't go to bed until 10:30 or 11 p.m. – "I don't want to miss anything," he said – and up again at 2.

"I catch up on my sleep in the winter," he said with a smile.

In an age when technology has made life easier in many ways and revolutionized the jobs we do and the way we do them, Tangier is one of those vanishing places where the watermen do things mostly the way they always have, or at least since the mid-1800s when working on the water began to replace farming as the island's primary occupation: Wake up before the sun. Get on a boat. Work long hours on the water, crabbing or oystering or fishing. Return home. Repeat the next day. And the next. At its best, the work is physically exhausting. At its worst, when there's little to catch, prices are dragging the bottom or the weather dreadful, it's emotionally defeating and even downright dangerous: eyes stung with the toxins of sea nettles, hands pierced with fishhooks, men lost when storms boil up and capsize boats. Sometimes the wind gusts so hard cabin windows on workboats are blown out and shatter, and the watermen wind up with facial lacerations. But this is what they know and love and choose to do, largely because their fathers and grandfathers and uncles did it, much like family farmers follow their personal tradition, through good harvests and bad. It provides a certain, reassuring rhythm to their lives. This is who they are. This is, at its most fundamental level, what it means to be a Tangierman.

Now, however, Tangiermen are disappearing. While the focus often is on the uncertain future of crabs and oysters – the oyster harvest from Virginia waters has rebounded in recent years from a low of 17,600 bushels in 1996 to more than 600,000 bushels in 2015-16, though it's nowhere near the historic highs of more than 4 million bushels a year in the middle 1950s – the watermen themselves are truly an endangered species.

"Just look at a waterman's hands," Nichols would tell anyone visiting Tangier for the first time who wanted to get to know the island. "You can tell so much. The cuts, the nicks, the partial amputations. Calluses all over the place. Just think of how hard these guys work."

He spoke out of pure admiration. The watermen's way of life was far removed from his, but their work ethic was something he could understand and appreciate, along with their devotion to tradition and their complete lack of pretension. Though his career and income allowed him to own a plane and several helicopters over the years, he felt a genuine kinship with the watermen.

However, every year fewer men on Tangier work the water for their livelihoods, victims of changing times, and the watermen will tell you, overzealous government regulations. Rules limit the number and size of crabs that can be caught, the length of the crabbing season and even the hours a waterman can work. In recent times, the state of Virginia has reduced the number of available crabbing licenses, and Tangier watermen said they have been particularly constrained by regulations in Virginia that are stricter than those in neighboring Maryland, the result of efforts by scientists and environmentalists wanting to boost sagging crab populations in the bay. But longtime watermen say crab populations, like other bay life, run in cycles. They also contend the impact of their work is far less of a problem than pollution in the bay that originates on the mainland. Throw in rising expenses and declining profits, and watermen are looking for other ways to make a living, which on Tangier often means having to leave the island. Some have gone to working on tugboats, jobs that carry good pay and benefits – an appealing prospect for self-employed watermen – but require long stretches away from home. Others have left the island altogether.

Eskridge – the nickname "Ooker" comes from his childhood when he crowed like the pet rooster that would follow him around, "Ooker" sounding a lot like "rooster" coming from the lips of a 4-year-old – has become more than a little familiar with the regulations and the plight of the watermen since taking over as Tangier's mayor in 2006 when his predecessor quit. He's come to know his way around not only pretty bay coves but also around the halls of state government and the offices of politicians. He's skeptical of the publicly enunciated reasons for stiffer regulations and suspects the bottom line might be that many of those in power would prefer the bay be used only for recreation.

"I don't have any problems with recreational fish-ing or crabbing on the bay," Eskridge said, "but I don't want them to put me out of business to do it. We don't want a handout. Just let us go to work and earn a living."

Eskridge, longtime mayor of Tangier, has become the face of the island in the halls of government.
Bob Brown/Richmond Times-Dispatch.

But this is not just business for Eskridge. It's very personal. He was only 4 or 5 years old when he started going out on the water with his father and grandfather, who also were watermen. Ask if there was ever any doubt he would choose this as his life's work, and the answer comes without pause: "Nope." He's been working full-time on the water since he graduated from the island's school.

With limited state licenses in demand, some waterman have sold theirs for tens of thousands of dollars and gotten out of the business. Not Eskridge. He has no price; he merely wants to "stay at it." Lean and deeply tanned, Eskridge, in his 50s, is a Tangierman through and through. He is eloquent in his advocacy of Tangier, but not overly talkative. He is friendly, but firm. He is deeply religious, which is obvious not just because he quotes freely from the Bible and has "Jesus" tattooed on his left forearm and a Star of David (to show his support for the people of Israel) on his right, but through the way he allows faith to direct his life. He is not showy in the least, though in the commercials for ESPN3 he did flash his dry sense of humor with the "Hook'em Horns" segment. He does not own a necktie.

"What you see is what you get," he said with a laugh. "For the governor, I'm going to put a better T-shirt on and a new pair of jeans."

For the messy work of crabbing he doesn't need to wear anything that nice. The most important articles of clothing might be his thick rubber gloves which save his fingers from not only the constant grappling with the wire pots but also from the pinching claws of crabs less than enthusiastic about being brought up from the bay floor. (He told a funny story about a visitor to an island crab shanty who apparently had little experience with crusta-

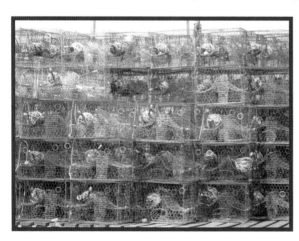

ceans, but wanted to hold a crab just the same. Ouch, he said. "I was watching his mouth," the visitor said, "but he bit me

Crab pots stacked on a dock.
Bill Lohmann

with his hands!") Oilskin overalls and boots complete his work attire.

As the sun rose higher in the morning sky, Eskridge slathered sunscreen on his tanned face and put on a less-than-trendy, broad-brimmed straw hat, joking that he was far enough from shore that no one could see him. As he moved his boat to the next crab pot, he reached into his small blue-and-white cooler and pulled out a sandwich. As he ate, he said he was irritated by those who cast watermen as anti-environment. No one knows the environment of the bay better than those who work on it every day, he said, and besides that, it doesn't make sense for watermen to overharvest crabs or do anything to spoil the most essential element of their livelihood.

"You have folks who condemn watermen, who say we want to catch the last crab," Eskridge said. "The resource is more valuable to me than anybody who studies it. I've got to put food on the table and put my daughter through college. Why would I want to catch the last crab?"

Eskridge said he loves this place too much to do anything to harm it. This is a man who resuscitates turtles that mistakenly swim into his crab pots. Whenever he pulls up a turtle that's been below the surface too long, he simply squeezes it gently and blows air into its nose a couple of times. Usually works like a charm.

Eskridge's roots run deep on Tangier. His mother
was a Pruitt, one of the families with the longest history
on the island. His father's family came to the island from
Fredericksburg, a mainland city about 90 miles west of
Tangier, around the time of the Civil War. They wanted
to get away from the war, he said, and they found like-
minded individuals on Tangier, which remained neutral
during the war. Tangiermen, Eskridge said, simply wanted to work. It is not unlike the watermen's wish today in
the face of what they deem as oppressive regulation.

The youngest of seven, Eskridge loves being his
own boss – "If I'm late a little bit, nobody hollers at me.
If I want to make it a shorter day, I can do it" – and he
adores working alone. Several workboats putter in the
distance, but otherwise Eskridge is by himself. Some
watermen like to work while surrounded by other watermen, and those fishing for hard crabs usually require a
larger boat, heavier traps and paid help. Hard-crabbing
is a more expensive proposition. Eskridge prefers the
solitude of soft-crabbing on a smaller boat. He cranks up
the volume on his radio to listen to the music and chatter
coming from a Christian station in Maryland. The sound
of a human voice through the speakers provides company, but he's just as happy listening to the soothing sounds
of wind and water and admiring the local bird population
that inhabit the islands and marshes: egrets, blue heron,
pelicans, eagles and osprey – called fish hawks by some
islanders. Eskridge figures he's installed more than 50 os-

prey stands around Tangier. He also enjoys the gulls that come calling pet-like, day-after-day, hoping Eskridge will toss them chunks of bait-fish, which he invariably does.

Eskridge joked that his appreciation of solitude can get him in trouble. On a mini-documentary produced for the island's museum, he mentioned that working in the seclusion of his crab shanty is a good place "to get away from it all."

"My wife saw it and said, 'Exactly what were you referring to? What do you mean?'" Eskridge said with a laugh.

Eskridge's wife, Irene, also a Tangier native, is a partner in one of the island's restaurants, Fisherman's Corner. They have six children, including four daughters adopted from India. Irene Eskridge always had considered adoption, her husband said, and the couple pursued that path after it was determined they couldn't have more biological children after their sons were born. Why India? A numbers of reasons, Eskridge said, including the fact adoptive parents were not required to travel to India to pick up the children. That kept expenses down. They adopted two girls and then two others who had been adopted by another American couple but were on the verge of being sent back to India. At the time of the interview, the youngest child attended Liberty University in the foothills of mainland Virginia. She doesn't have an Indian accent, as Eskridge said, she has a Tangier accent. Her name, Sreedevi, is also the name of his boat.

"Takes a lot of crabs to put somebody through college," Eskridge said, noting the house is finally growing quiet after almost 30 years of children padding about. He said with a laugh that coming up with college tuition might not have been the most challenging aspect of his household. What might that have been? "Sharing a house with four teenage girls and one bathroom."

As mayor, Eskridge has had to confront far thornier issues, such as a dwindling population and the disappearance of the island itself. By one estimate, Tangier is losing an estimated nine acres of land a year. At that rate, the island will be gone within a century, perhaps even decades sooner. While crabbing, Eskridge pointed to slivers of land that were once full-size islands. A row of power lines that stretch through the water hundreds of yards from one island originally were erected along the edge of the island. The shore has receded that much. It's clear the $300 Eskridge is paid each month to be mayor is not nearly enough.

A study published in December 2015 in Scientific Reports said the combination of erosion and sea-level rise – a "double-whammy," according to one of the report's authors, David M. Schulte, a marine biologist for the U.S. Army Corps of Engineers – had reduced Tangier's land mass by more than half since 1850. The way things were going, the report stated, Tangier residents might have to abandon their homes within 50 years.

Schulte said Tangier and the other islands in the Chesapeake are made of sand and peat deposits from marshland vegetation, rather than stone, making them more vulnerable to "big changes" when storms roll through the bay. Unlike a shifting barrier island that has a constant supply of sand for replenishment, Tangier has no such benefit.

"When it erodes away," Schulte said, "it's gone."

The report flatly stated that Tangier was "running out of time, and if no action is taken, the citizens of Tangier may become among the first climate change refugees in the continental USA."

Cognizant of their dire prospect but also defiant in the face of what might await them, Tangier residents seized upon the "refugee" part of the report and began selling T-shirts imprinted with "I refuse to be a climate change refugee." Their defiance is derived in part from the fact they do not generally believe in the notion of human-caused climate change, therefore doubting that premise within the report. (Most, though not all, believe erosion is primarily to blame, and jetties or seawalls are the principle solution.)

Nonetheless, sea level in the bay has been rising slowly for the past 5,000 years at the rate of about a foot per century, said Carlton H. Hershner Jr., director of the Center for Coastal Resources Management for the Virginia Institute of Marine Science. A combination of climate change and local geology – the water is coming up, the land is going down, a phenomenon known as subsidence – will doom Tangier, as it has doomed smaller islands already, he said.

Subsidence – the actual sinking of the island – is caused in the region, according to the study published in Scientific Reports, by "glacial rebound," resulting from the melting of the ice sheet that once covered much of northern North America, groundwater extraction and the effects of a meteor impact in the southern Chesapeake Bay millions of years ago.

In fact, a tide gauge maintained by the National Oceanic and Atmospheric Administration at Lewisetta, Va., near where the Potomac River meets the bay, shows the combination of rising waters and subsidence has raised sea level about 5 millimeters a year since 1970 -- a rate of more than a foot a century.

Dr. Lynton S. Land, a geologist who lives nearby on the mainland of Virginia, said Tangier's fate is a foregone conclusion.

"Nothing can be done about it," he said in early 2018. "It's just a question of 'When?'"

He said the scientific conclusion that sea level is rising is "a fact." While there also is erosion, Land said "erosion is caused by rising sea level.

"There is absolutely zero chance that is wrong," said Land, a professor emeritus of the Jackson School of Geosciences at the University of Texas at Austin who moved to the community of Ophelia on the Northern Neck almost 20 years ago after retiring.

The only "wild card," in his view, is if the island will be gradually swamped by rising sea levels or wiped out by a monster storm, such as the hurricane of 1933 that for decades was used as a measure of destruction on the island. In that storm, according to an Associated Press report at the time, more than 60 boats were damaged or lost and numerous crab processing plants – when such enterprises existed on the island – were damaged or destroyed. That storm inundated Tangier, driving some residents to the top floors of their homes. Others fled to the safety of the mainland and never returned, beginning a steady decline of the island's population, which stood at 1,120 in 1930, according to the U.S. Census.

A storm of such magnitude now would have the potential of causing even more damage on Tangier since there is so much less of the island than there was in 1933. More recently, the winds and rain of Hurricane Isabel (2003) and Hurricane Sandy (2012) pushed seawater onto Tangier streets, damaged homes and destroyed crab shacks along the harbor.

In his 2005 book, "The Disappearing Islands of the Chesapeake," author William B. Cronin chronicles the similar plight of dozens of islands in the bay, including Maryland's Holland Island, west of Salisbury. A community thrived on Holland Island for the better part of a century. Men made their livelihoods from crabs in the summer and oysters in the winter, and families sustained themselves by raising much of their own food. There was a school, a church and a post office, as well as a few shops. The island even had a baseball team. In 1900, the 250 residents who lived on Holland Island could not envision having to abandon their homes, Cronin wrote.

But erosion was eating away at the island, and those who lived there saw just how relentless the winds and waves – and time – could be. By 1910, Cronin wrote, many islanders had relocated to the mainland, and the island's preacher, postmaster and physician were gone. A summer gale in 1918 drove the last family away. By the 1940s, the only residents were songbirds, blue herons and seagulls on what little was left of the island. By 2000, a single house remained, and its image was featured on the back jacket of Cronin's book. The outline of the baseball diamond was still visible, as were the tombstones of the island's cemetery, which, Cronin wrote, "were surrounded in a watery field of marsh grass."

Holland Island's story sounds eerily similar to Tangier's.

A portending example of what might await Tangier is a place called Uppards – the name came from its location "upwards" of the island – a one-time section of Tangier across the island's primary channel that until the early 1900s was a vibrant, self-sufficient community with homes and footbridges connecting to the main island. Uppards, known originally among residents as Canaan, had three little neighborhoods and markets but no church, so every Sunday the residents would make three trips across the channel on the narrow footbridge that had no railings – three trips because the island's only church at that time held morning, afternoon and evening services. In the winter, residents would toss coal cinders on the icy bridge so they wouldn't slip into the frigid water. Sometimes the ice was too thick and slick for the cinders to do any good, and stories are told of the most faithful residents of Uppards crawling across the slippery bridge when it was too treacherous to walk. Alas, there is little left of Uppards, and the last residents left the island by the 1930s.

By 2016, Uppards was a deserted patch of marshland with little visible beyond a few gravestones that had washed up on its sliver of a beach. The bay has claimed most everything else.

Carol Moore, who grew up on Tangier, came along well after Uppards had been abandoned, yet she feels a strong connection to the place. As often as she can, Moore motors her skiff through the Tangier harbor and follows the shoreline around to the far end of Uppards. Bittersweet as those visits are, she said Uppards is her favorite place on earth.

"I've been going to Uppards since I was a little child with my father," said Moore, whose uncle owned a hunting lodge on Uppards. "I was up there all the time. I remember when it used to be filled with fig trees, maple trees, walnut trees and flowers, goats and chickens. I remember the land being so big and wide and high and long. In the 1970s, we didn't get to travel very much. It was like when you left Tangier to go to Uppards you were in a whole other world."

In October 2012, Hurricane Sandy flooded homes on Tangier, ripped up docks, destroyed a crab shanty and sunk several boats. The next day, Moore ventured to Uppards. When she walks the beach at Uppards, she routinely finds a variety of shells, occasionally arrowheads and often artifacts from long-ago lives on Uppards: bricks and wood from homes that have washed away and even an occasional bathroom sink. After Hurricane Sandy, she found something altogether different and alarming: a human skull rolling around in the surf.

"I was like, 'Oh, Lord!' Then when I looked more there were at least three complete skeletons on the surface," Moore recalled. "It bothered me, so I stayed three or four hours just contemplating ... just feeling sad for the people and Uppards."

She returned home and called authorities. Archaeologists with the Virginia Department of Historic Resources (DHR) recovered five sets of remains and identified them as four adults and a child, a girl estimated to have been 3 to 5 years old. The coffin hardware and other artifacts found with the remains indicated the individuals were likely buried in the very late 1800s or early 1900s, said Joanna Wilson Green, an archaeologist with DHR. The remains were cleaned, conserved and analyzed before being transferred to the Smithsonian Institution where they were held until residents of Tangier determined whether they wanted to rebury them on the island.

"It almost feels like when I go to Uppards, I'm taking a journey into my past, but when I take my grandchildren, it's like I'm taking a trek into their future," Moore said. "My past was secure with Tangier. Their future is not secure, and every time I go I have mixed feelings. I remember the life I had on Uppards and Tangier, and when I go I try to imagine what it will be like for my grandchildren not to have Tangier and Uppards."

As the remainder of Uppards goes away, so too does the last natural line of protection of Tangier's harbor from the open waters of the bay, putting workboats and crab houses in peril, as well as the island itself.

"The reality is," Schulte told me for an interview with the Richmond Times-Dispatch in May 2016, "without Uppards you're not going to have Tangier."

The "sad truth," Schlute said, is that Tangier "is going away. The action that has to save it has not been initiated. They've still got some time, but they're running out."

That action includes an initial step of constructing a 500-foot-long jetty along one edge of the Uppards at the ever-widening mouth of the channel that leads into Tangier's increasingly exposed harbor, which is the center of the island's economy. The jetty was proposed by the Army Corps of Engineers in 1996 and remained under discussion and study for two decades as the corps – and the island – waited for available funding. Eskridge called the long delay "discouraging. There are folks who would like to invest here in a business or their homes, and it's just they hesitate to do it because if the help doesn't come, especially those near the shoreline, they're going to be in trouble."

The jetty finally appeared to be on the horizon in early 2018 when a spokesman for the Norfolk office of the Corps of Engineers said construction likely would begin on the $2.4 million project in the federal government's fiscal year 2019, meaning after Oct. 1, 2018.

A seawall constructed on the southwestern side of the island in the 1980s has saved Tangier's airstrip, which had been in danger of washing away.
Bob Brown/Richmond Times-Dispatch

However, the proposed jetty represents only a partial remedy at best. More such barriers would be required to give Tangier a chance to survive. The Scientific Reports study suggested construction of a series of segmented breakwaters around much of the island, as well as the creation of a sand beach and dune system along the western edge of the island between the breakwaters and the existing shoreline. The study also suggested building up island marches with dredged sand and new plantings of loblolly pines to maintain elevation. Such projects had not been formally studied or proposed – much less funded. The report's authors estimated the total cost would be at least $20 million.

Money. Tangier doesn't have a lot of it, and the notion of spending millions on a speck of land with a insecure future is a tough sell for those who don't know the island (and maybe even for those who do). A common refrain among mainlanders: Help Tangiermen relocate to the mainland, but don't throw public funds at a place that might be going away anyway; it's not worth the gamble.

"Man, I get steamed when I hear that," said Eskridge, the mayor. "They don't understand our way of life. We've been here for hundreds of years."

In June 2017, Eskridge was stunned when President Trump phoned him after watching a CNN report on the island that mentioned how Tangier residents had voted overwhelmingly for Trump in the 2016 presidential election. Eskridge said on the CNN report that he loved Trump as much as he would a family member.

Eskridge told *The Daily Times* of Salisbury, Md., that Trump told him, "You've got one heck of an island there."

"He said not to worry about sea-level rise," Eskridge said. "He said, 'Your island has been there for hundreds of years, and I believe your island will be there for hundreds more.'"

Trump's reassurance notwithstanding, Tangier needs a lot of help to survive.

For many Tangiermen, the island is where they were born and where they intend to die. They cannot

"Ooker" Eskridge and others routinely gather to discuss the island's future as they did here in 2016 in a back room of the old clinic.
Bob Brown/Richmond Times-Dispatch

fathom giving up on a place like that, and they are willing to take whatever chances are necessary to save their home and their heritage, and they figure they have earned government help. It bothers Tangiermen that the United States sees no problem, in an example Eskridge cited, financing the construction of bridges and roads in nations such as Iraq, but balks at finding money to preserve an American town with 400 years of history and tradition. He said when called, Tangier has sacrificed for the country. Nine Tangiermen were killed during World War II. In Vietnam, one Tangierman didn't come home: Warren Reed Eskridge, brother of Mayor Ooker Eskridge.

"The watermen here don't ask for a lot," Eskridge said. "We lose crab pots and crab houses from storms, but we don't ask to be compensated by the government. We just bear it and keep going. But what we need now is out of our reach. We can't do anything about it. We'd like some help from the government."

Tangier residents point to the success of a seawall that was constructed on the southwestern side of the island in the 1980s. The wall of boulders saved the island's airstrip, which had lost about 600 feet in length in the four decades since it was built and was in danger of being washed away entirely, cutting off a necessary link to the world.

"We were losing 20 or 25 feet a year in shoreline there," Eskridge said. "They completed that in '89, and we haven't lost one inch since, so it works."

Tangiermen are further perturbed because of extensive projects in the bay such as the $9 million "living shoreline" constructed last year at Glen Martin National Wildlife Refuge, a dozen miles to the north of Tangier, just across the Maryland state line. There, the U.S. Fish and Wildlife Service used sand, rock and boulders to create almost four miles of barrier to protect the marsh, which is home to an array of migratory birds. No one lives at the refuge, though the work likely will benefit adjacent Smith Island, which faces a similar plight as Tangier and in 2016 was home to fewer than 300 people.

"They put enough stone up there that you could have circled (Tangier) with it almost," Eskridge said. "It's people that need the help and not ducks."

Man-made jetties and breakwaters or not, Eskridge believes the outcome – good or bad – is out of the islanders' control.

"That's in God's hands," the mayor said. "If He wants the island here, then nothing can take it away. If He doesn't really want it here, I don't know."

In the wake of all of the perilous news, Tangier Island was officially designated in 2015 as a historic district on the Virginia Landmarks Register and is now included on the National Register of Historic Places. Marc Wagner, architectural historian for the Virginia Department of Historic Resources, conducted the research that led to the historic district designation and fell in love with the island.

"It's like no place I've been in Virginia," Wagner said. "The architecture is important ... (but) we don't just look at the architecture. You have the architecture that's there plus the cultural history, and you've got something that's very special."

Wagner grew up in a coastal village in Connecticut so he "felt sort of home" when he visited Tangier where the vast majority of families rely on the bay for their livelihoods.

"It's just really unusual to be immersed in that, where there is that single purpose," he said. "They live by the rhythms of the bay."

Wagner said it's painful to imagine the world without Tangier.

"It strikes at my heart because it's such a special place," he said, "for Virginia and for the whole bay."

Eskridge motored across the cove and pulled alongside the deadrise skippered by his buddy Dan Dise, who was crab-scraping – essentially dredging the bottom for crabs as his boat crept through the water. In his 30s at the time, Dise was one of the youngest working watermen. While most of his contemporaries sought out other livelihoods, Dise felt a calling to work on the water. He spent his early years on Maryland's Smith Island, about a dozen miles north of Tangier; his mother was from Smith, his father from Tangier. There were watermen on both sides of his family, including his father. When his parents divorced, he moved with his mother to the Maryland mainland and stayed there until his teen years. He loved playing baseball, but as an outsider, he detested dealing with the cliques on the mainland. He spent summers on Tangier and knew that was where he belonged.

"I did good in school, but I hated it," said Dise, president of the Tangier Watermen's Association. "I knew I didn't want to go to college. I worked with my dad every summer, and I enjoyed it. I just knew I wanted to do it."

In the summer of 2014, Dise was still president of the Tangier Watermen's Association – "or what's left of it," he said. There were maybe 60 working watermen on Tangier, compared to well more than 100 not that many years earlier, he said. As many men work off the island on tugs as work on the water. Regular meetings of the association have become more like informal gatherings at the Tangier Oil Co. (a combination fueling station, hardware store and public square known locally as the Dock Store) where Dise shares the latest from the Virginia Marine Resources Commission or any other information that needs dissemination. Word of mouth takes care of the rest.

"When I started there were 70-some people who shedded crabs," said Dise. "Now there's about 20. It's just unreal how many people have gotten out of it."

With a wife and two children, he had no plans to join them.

"I'm too stupid to do anything else," he said with a laugh. "I love it."

Full-time watermen generally chase crabs from April through November, then oysters through the bitter cold days of winter. March is reserved for getting their gear ready for the next season and recharging their own batteries – and hoping the future will look brighter by then.

By early afternoon, a few minutes before state law said he had to finish harvesting his crabs, Eskridge hoisted, dumped and replaced the last of his crab pots. He steered his boat to a clump of land, rinsed himself and his gear with buckets of bay water, and then headed back to Tangier with a good day's catch. As he slowed the engine and entered Tangier's harbor, Eskridge eased his boat past the rows of crab shanties, a number of which were no longer in use, some of them shuttered with "For Sale" signs, more evidence of the uncertain times ahead for the island and its mayor.

In 2016, Tangier resident Lonnie Moore walks past tombstones on the beach at Uppards, a once-thriving community on the island that has been overtaken by the Chesapeake Bay in the last century.
Bob Brown/Richmond Times-Dispatch

Nichols with Kim Clark (left) and Tess Owens play with the Nichols' dog, Teddy, in May 2007.
Dianne Nichols

SEVEN

HEADMASTER AND TASKMASTER
'There's no such word as 'can't' '

*T*alk to anyone who ever worked for or with David Nichols, and eventually they almost always come around to comparing the experience to an education – specifically as students enrolled in the make-believe but in some ways very real Nichols School of Hard Knocks, presided over by Nichols himself, the stern headmaster delivering valuable instruction, lifelong lessons and tough love.

His staff even gave Nichols a card-holder with a gold plaque that read: "Nichols School of Hard Knocks."

"You remember your parents telling you when you had a hard teacher in school and they said the days may be hard but you're going to learn a lot more from a harder teacher than one who was easier?" said Rhonda Lawrence, one of the first nurses he hired at his White

Stone practice. "That was very true of David. He was a wonderful teacher. He taught me the true meaning of treating each patient like they were your mother or father or brother or sister. That's how he treated every one of his patients, and that's why he became our family physician. He even helped deliver our second son since he was still doing maternity care in the early '80s."

"I learned everything from the Nichols School of Hard Knocks," said Beth Somers, who wasn't a nurse when Nichols hired her but became one under his guidance. "He was a great teacher. He wanted it done right, and he wanted it done right every time. Details were very, very important. Everything I learned from him I've carried with me."

Riggs, the physician assistant who worked for Nichols in the early 1980s, signed a letter more than a quarter-century later, "Allan Riggs, alumnus of the David B. Nichols School of Hard Knocks, class of 1985."

"He could be very intense at times, but he was a very good physician," said Riggs, who went on to work as a physician assistant at Central Michigan University where he also taught in the physician assistant program. "I will always remember David's care and concern for his patients. I learned a lot that I still use to this day in my practice, and I have shared many of the medical pearls I learned from him with my PA students. David has influenced many PAs he never met."

Riggs remembered Nichols as "a fun guy to work with," which was true, but he also could be difficult. For those who knew Nichols only in passing, he appeared kindly, obliging and soft-spoken – and he was all of those things – but he also was hard-charging, demanding and, as Riggs said, intense.

He was a great delegator but, according to those who worked for him, something of a control freak – at one point, he gave his nurses two-way radios in the office so they could be working on assigned tasks but also could be within the press of a button if he needed to summon them instantly or if he simply wanted to know where they were – and in subtle and not-so-subtle ways, a great motivator. He saw potential in others they often didn't see in themselves and invested in his staff considerable faith that evolved into high expectations.

"As soon as I would start to say, 'I can't,' he'd say, 'Make it happen,'" said Cindy Parks, who was born and raised on Tangier and became a longtime office assistant at the island clinic, having been invited to work there even though she doubted she was cut out for the job. "I know he caused me to do a lot of things I wouldn't have done just because he wouldn't let me say I couldn't do it."

As an aside, Parks was one of two Cindys in the small office. The other was Cindy Wheatley, a phlebotomist who worked as a laboratory technician, and they would both answer whenever Nichols would call "Cindy!" So, using their job duties as a guide, he nicknamed Parks "Cindy Money" and Wheatley "Cindy Blood."

"At first I didn't like it," Parks said, "but it was kind of an endearment, I guess."

Nichols had grown up with high expectations placed upon him by his father, so it really had become the way he operated. He cared deeply about what people thought about him, and he cared just as intensely, if not more, about his patients, and that combination was the driving force in the way he worked and the way he managed – whether the issue was a patient's examination or the tidiness of the office.

"Everything he did, he wanted perfection," said Kim Clark, the office manager at the White Stone practice. "He was very structured and driven, and he knew how to run a tight ship."

In his pursuit of perfection, however, results often fell short, and he could be quick-tempered with his staff and less than diplomatic, more focused on goals, ideals and the bottom line.

"I learned after many years that his bark was worse than his bite," Clark said.

Rhonda Lawrence met Nichols in 1981 when he was still moonlighting one weekend a month at the Kilmarnock hospital's emergency room.

"Our young son was sick and not improving so we went to the ER to have him evaluated," Lawrence recalled. "(Nichols) found out I was an LPN, and he was looking for an office nurse, and after an interview I was hired and became an employee of White Stone Family Practice, working both full and part time for the next 18 years."

Lawrence and Clark often commuted to work together. They were expected to arrive at the office at least 15 minutes before patients started arriving. However, there were rare occasions they ran late, so they would be on the lookout for him on their drive. If they saw him running along the road – he loved to jog in the mornings – they would be "safe," Lawrence said with a laugh, and they would be able to get everything ready the way he liked it. If they didn't see him, though, he might already be at the office, and well, that was just problematic.

The early days were hard, she said."I can't sugar-coat it."

In a new practice with a young physician, the hours were long and the work was demanding -- just like Nichols.The employees had to take their vacations when Nichols took his because, as Lawrence recalled, "That's just the way it was."

She was a young mother who had to pick up her son by a certain time at the babysitter. Many times, Clark would leave and pick him up while Lawrence finished with patient care. Lawrence said she respected Nichols, but that she too could be stubborn and didn't mind standing up for herself.

"I didn't always accept the 'Word of David' the same as the 'Word of God," she said.

After she left the practice and moved from the area, she would occasionally drop by the office to say hello to Nichols and Clark, and they would talk about the old days and joke about how they had mellowed with age. As an early graduate of Nichols' "School of Hard Knocks," Lawrence said she was well-prepared for her next career as an office manager for a busy family practice office in Northern Virginia.

Nichols acknowledged that he was demanding, but he also said he mellowed over the years and explained, "Whatever I demanded was for the betterment of patient care. I had to create a standard and constantly live up to it. I didn't accept anything less."

Newman, the other physician in the practice, witnessed Nichols' genuine care for his patients from the beginning. Newman, who would work as Nichols' associate in the practice for more than 15 years, visited White Stone in 1984 to interview for the job and saw the way Nichols operated.

On a Sunday morning, Nichols and Newman had gone to the office to meet an elderly woman with emphysema to evaluate her cough and shortness of breath.

"He helped her from the car and held her hand and walked her into the office," Newman recalled. "He spent over an hour patiently evaluating her problems, including doing the chest X-ray himself and prescribing appropriate therapy. He was always gentle and kind with his patients."

The following year, Newman filled in at the White Stone practice for a week so Nichols could take a vacation, something he'd seldom done since he opened the practice. Newman remembered that period, with a laugh, as "my trial by fire."

In 1986, Newman completed his seven-year obligation to the Navy, and Nichols hired him. In the Navy, Newman had worked as an attending doctor in a residency program, a side of medicine he loved. He wanted to work in a "full-spectrum practice," where he could gain a richly diverse experience before returning to the academic world and going into teaching. He found just what he was looking for in White Stone: a practice that, as he put it, "did house calls and cradle-to-grave care." They delivered babies – Nichols laughed about the time one of his patients went into labor while he was at a movie theater in Gloucester and received a beep on his pager indicating the film was over for him – and visited the homes of terminally ill patients too sick to come to the office, and they maintained weekend hours. And on Thursdays, they traveled to Tangier. For years, they alternated Thursday trips to Tangier – Nichols and Newman – hiring local pilots to fly Newman back and forth from the island, although Nichols himself did the flying on occasion to deliver his associate to Tangier. On Nichols' Thursdays, of course, he piloted himself.

The arrival of Newman took immense pressure off Nichols, who concluded that he had devoted too much of himself to his practice and not enough to his young family. He also had begun to wear down from not having another physician in the practice to help cover the Saturdays and the generally long hours that running a solo practice entails, and from essentially always being on call. In a small community, it was not unusual for patients to show up at his house with medical needs. He remembered the time someone arrived in his driveway with a bleeding finger. He often would return to the office with the patients, unless it was something he could take care of at home or standing in his driveway.

"What are you going to do?" Nichols said in a 2010 interview of his early years in practice. "I would see people in my office seven, eight, nine, 10 times a weekend. I would get called all the time, and I felt like I had to do that. Turns out a lot of doctors in the area were relying on the (hospital) emergency room. I was young, and I felt like I had to build the practice and do it right. I wanted to be all things to my patients."

Nichols and Newman set about establishing a way of operating the practice that Newman believes was a model of what years later became known in healthcare reform circles as a "patient-centered medical home."

"Things like open access, being available, coverage after hours, making arrangements for your patients to see consultants you would see yourself, those kinds of things," Newman said. "That's what I feel we were doing during the golden years in White Stone and Tangier… to serve the population and to be patient-friendly."

At the core of it all was Nichols' overall diligence and attention to detail. "One of the most thorough physicians I've ever known," Newman said.

Duffer, the physician assistant who worked in Nichols' practice for almost two decades, said Nichols and Newman "taught me a whole lot."

"That's what attracted me to the practice, the way they did it," said Duffer, who was retired from the Army and had been deployed to Iraq during Operation Desert Storm with the 101st Airborne. "If you had a patient, you took care of them. You spent time with them.

"I liked the style of practice, and I liked the intensity and the thoroughness. That's what made (Nichols) successful."

Nichols' meticulous approach pervaded the entire operation, not just patient care. As a businessman, he was always focused on the bottom line and consumed with getting the best deal possible – down to the price of cotton balls.

Somers was in charge of ordering supplies during her time at the practice, and whenever the invoice would arrive for any supplies, she knew by the end of the day Nichols would buzz the front desk and summon her to account for the price.

He would run the list of items, ask about each price – including cotton balls – and ask if the price was the same as it was last month. And if it wasn't, why wasn't it? And if there was a new item on the list, he would ask why she purchased that brand. "Well, because they're so much cheaper per dozen," she might say.

"I had to justify every item," Somers said. "If the price of a certain item had gone up considerably from the last time I ordered, the next morning I had to get those people on the phone and ask, 'Why is it $12 more?'"

Somers went to work for Nichols in 1983, having left a job in research and development that she had grown not to enjoy. A friend suggested she talk to Nichols, who needed a nurse. "But I'm not a nurse," Somers said. Her friend said talk to him anyway.

Nichols hired her and proceeded to teach her everything about a medical practice. She learned to take X-rays and draw blood and conduct myriad medical tests. She also maintained the schedules and, of course, ordered supplies.

"It was all hands-on," she said. "There was nothing greater for him than to have a patient come in … (and) he would stick his head out of the room and see who was out there. 'Come in here! Have you ever seen such and such before?'

"There were huge life lessons," said Somers, who worked two different stints for Nichols, spanning well over a decade before going on to teach music at Chesapeake Academy in Irvington. "When you reported … back to him, he made sure you had all of your details right. It has helped me with everything I do: the details and thinking it through to the next step and not letting things drop through the cracks. We would butt heads every now and then, but in the end the things he taught me I will carry forever."

Trained as a licensed practical nurse, Lawrence said she had taken classes involving the dispensing of medicine and performing intravenous therapy, but she never envisioned doing X-rays or blood tests until she started working for Nichols. His on-the-job instruction was more effective and lasting than anything she had previously experienced.

"The first time I drew blood, he guided my hand," she recalled. "Then he said, 'Next time, you can do it.'"

Staffers joked that you dared not call in sick because Nichols, who didn't much care for having his routine upended, might make a house call on you and see if he could make you well enough to work. And his unyielding reputation was known beyond the office walls. Tess Owens, who worked for Nichols for 13 years and, along with Kim Clark and Inez Pruitt, comprised "The Three Musketeers," as dubbed by Nichols, said she and others dropped Nichols' name on occasion when calling other physicians' offices for referrals or tests or almost anyplace – even the electric company when it wanted to shut off power for a brief period because of some special work in the area. If they weren't making headway with what they needed, they were known to say, "Do you realize I'm Dr. David Nichols' nurse?!?" More often than not, it worked – and the power never was shut off. Owens said with a laugh she had been tempted to inject the same phrase at restaurants when the wait was long, but she never had the nerve.

If Nichols was demanding in the way he dealt with his staff, he was altogether fierce when it came to conducting business. He was relentless – perhaps even slightly ruthless – when negotiating for the lowest price on just about everything, from cotton balls to helicopters to real estate.

Riggs, the physician assistant, marveled at Nichols' thriftiness and business skills.

"I would squirm when he negotiated with a medical equipment salesman," Riggs said. "David would tell him to sharpen his pencil and then proceed to get a fantastic, discounted price along with a few years supply of free paper for the EKG machine."

Andy Gibbs, of Hampton Roads Helicopters, sold Nichols five helicopters over the years and taught him to fly them. (In addition, Nichols also attended safety school in California after the acquisition of each new helicopter.) Nichols had initiated the relationship, having read a magazine article about a particular kind of helicopter and called Gibbs, who told him he probably didn't want one of those, but they could get together and chat about other possibilities.

"I didn't have any idea I was about to create a monster," Gibbs said with a laugh.

Nichols always wanted the newest model because of the updated warranty, so he was quite willing to trade in his used chopper, but that didn't mean he was any sort of pushover on making a deal. In fact, Gibbs recalled negotiations with Nichols were always "a process."

"I'd get him up to about 1 percent above cost, and I'd say, 'David, that's just not enough to pay the bills,'" Gibbs said.

Newman recalled the sales representative who spent a half-hour in Nichols' office discussing the final price of a treadmill for the practice, finally emerging with "beads of sweat on his forehead and armpits soaked with perspiration. He said, 'I just sold the treadmill for below my cost.'"

"David was an incredibly tough business person," said Newman, who knew first-hand from his own contract negotiations with him. "He angered a lot of people and made some enemies. He was very, very, very effective in terms of negotiating skills. I don't know where he learned it, but he had it. And he could usually get what he wanted. He wasn't mean or ugly about it. He never raised his voice. He was just persistent until he got what he wanted."

It was all just part of his thoroughness in the way he approached everything. "A complex guy," Newman said.

Neighbors considered Nichols friendly, if somewhat reserved until you got to know him. Michael York, a Northern Virginia resident who owns a river home about a half-mile from the Nichols, first came to know Nichols' father, an avid walker who lived in a house next door to David and Dianne in his later years. York was always walking his dogs, and Nichols' father was always walking. Later, York got to know David.

"David was somebody everybody knew, at least by reputation," York said – and by the fact he often landed his helicopter at his house.

Nichols and York hit it off, in part because York also was a pilot, though he didn't fly helicopters. An attorney, York also had a particularly deep appreciation for Nichols' work. In his earlier life, York was a Pulitzer Prize-winning investigative reporter for the Lexington (Ky.) Herald-Leader and later The Washington Post. Along the way, he covered medicine for a couple of years and won numerous awards for an investigation of nation-wide mortality rates for heart-bypass operations.

What struck York about Nichols as a physician – and at one point York's mother, a stroke victim, was a patient of his – was his thoroughness and the way he thought "a good doctor should be a good scientist."

"I was really lucky I got to know some world-famous docs, and you could put David right up there in terms of how he approached his practice. This is a small town," York said of White Stone, "but he was as good a doctor as you could expect to find anywhere."

Dr. Neil S. Kaye, a psychiatrist, came to the same conclusion about Nichols.

"He was absolutely a first-rate physician," Kaye said. "His clinical knowledge was vast, his experience was fabulous, but his attitude of going to find the problem and the source – 'I'm not going to just treat symptoms, I'm going to get to the bottom of things' – was unbelievable.

"In the world of physicians, he was in the top 10 percent. Maybe 5 percent. What he did with that old (clinic) was nothing short of miraculous. He was working out of something that was only one step above a MASH army tent, saving lives and keeping people going in an incredible way. People didn't realize how good a doc he was. If he lived in Wilmington, that's who I'd go to as my family doc. In a heartbeat."

Kaye and his wife, Dr. Susan Kaye, a pathologist, lived part-time on Tangier for seven years, commuting on weekends from their home in Wilmington, Del. Their mode of transportation? Neil's helicopter.

"We shared medicine and flying helicopters," Kaye said of his friendship with Nichols. "Even down to the same model helicopter. At one point, our helicopters were seven serial numbers apart. They were made the same week!"

Nichols and the Kayes consulted on cases, and Neil flew a number of Nichols' patients to Crisfield for dialysis, broken arms and other non-trauma events.

"He was humble and not afraid to say, 'I don't know as much as I wish I did on this topic,'" Neil Kaye said. "He really just believed in helping people and in doing what he felt was right. He set very high standards for everyone around him, no higher than he would set for himself."

Aside from speaking of the "Nichols School of Hard Knocks," everyone who worked any length of time for him talked, like Owens, about the way he "took me under his wing."

"This is truly where I learned things like 'The patient comes first, not sometimes but always;' 'There's no such word as 'can't;' 'Make it happen;' and my most favorite, 'Always get four vital signs,'" said Owens, the last one being problematic, she added, because in the course of ascertaining four vital signs, nurses invariably would be "interrupted by you know who."

The funny thing was Nichols knew he was that way and tried to mitigate any longstanding hard feelings by telling those who worked for him what he told Owens early on in her employment: "Never take anything he said during the day home with me. After a few years I learned to do that."

As hard-charging as he was with his employees in the office, he often treated them like family outside it. Lawrence said when she was diagnosed with breast cancer years after leaving the practice and moving from the area, Nichols was among the first people from her old hometown to call her. When Riggs arrived for an interview in White Stone, he stayed as a guest at the Nichols home while he worked several days at the clinic to see if the job was a good match. Riggs said he also appreciated that Nichols offered to advance him his salary those first few weeks knowing his budget had been strained by the move.

Riggs saw that sort of care and concern for patients. Not just the thoroughness that Nichols was known for but his evenhanded approach to caring for all. The most poignant example Riggs could recall occurred the day he was examining a black patient, an older man, in the early 1980s, not that far removed from the days of segregation and separate and often unequal medical care.

"I was getting real close to the patient's face to examine the retina in the back of his eye with an ophthalmoscope," Riggs said, "and this man looked up at me and said, 'You know that's one reason I like to see you doctors. You're not afraid to touch a colored person.'

"That really hit me and it almost brings tears to my eyes even now," Riggs said nearly 30 years later. "I guess he'd been to a practice where the doctor wouldn't touch him. David saw everybody. He just had a great practice, and the people really loved him."

Nichols always remained obsessed on the bottom line, but Newman said he believed his focus widened in later years, becoming "more mission-oriented. Between his real estate developing business and the practice, he had made as much money as he needed," Newman said.

"We used to go to his place at the beach for a long weekend for practice-planning seminars," Newman said. "He and I would talk business and talk about the five- and 10-year plan for the practice. He told me one time he wished he could throw all the financial stuff away and become a missionary physician, Doctors Without Borders kind of guy. To hell with all the financial stuff. He was a masterful business operator ... but I think that was his secret fantasy deep-down wish."

In fact, Nichols used to think he had become too detached from the world of need by practicing in White Stone, which he felt was almost "country club medicine" compared to places where the need for medical care was desperate and more basic. He was afraid he had become too insulated and wasn't appropriately using the gift of a medical education he had been given. Then he remembered he was sharing his gift and had been for years on Tangier Island.

"I realized what I was doing on Tangier was pretty sacrificial in many ways ... that what I was doing across the Chesapeake was like going across the Atlantic. I do believe there is an awful lot people can do in their own backyard without having to go all over the world."

His goal became not only doing that work on Tangier, but ensuring it would continue after he was gone. He didn't want the residents of Tangier to have to scramble for medical care the way they did in the years before he arrived. That's why he pushed his assistants to learn all they could. With the labor shared, they could care for more patients. It helped lighten his load, but it also empowered those he taught, both off the island and on. People like Inez Pruitt.

Nichols, at the helicopter pad in his front yard, ready for work and flight in 2006. *Nichols family*

On a visit to the old clinic in August 2010, Nichols chats up visitors in the waiting room while Pruitt makes a phone call from the office.
Bob Brown/Richmond Times-Dispatch

EIGHT

'A Lady Dr. Nichols'
'Do I want this job?'

*E*lizabeth "Inez" Parks Pruitt is a true child of Tangier. She was born in 1962 in a house centrally located on the small island: a walk of 100 yards or so to Swain United Methodist Church, the island's schoolhouse and the post office, and maybe in a flash of divine foreshadowing, next door to the property that would become, almost five decades later, the site of the island's health center.

Her mother was a homemaker, her father a waterman and a character who owned the local marina and called everybody "George." The middle of five children, she grew up fearlessly navigating small boats around the island and swimming in the tidal creeks that meander throughout the island.

"I don't remember learning to swim," she said. "I've always *known* how to swim."

And she always knew, deep down, she wanted to be a nurse.

"We had a doctor coming over from the Eastern Shore," she said. "Dr. White. People called him 'Ike.' He would come almost every Wednesday or Thursday when I was really small, and he would stay at our house. I couldn't have been more than 5 or 6 years old, but he would let me go on house calls with him. I was just so curious, and I was so taken with what he did. I wanted to be a nurse and help people get well."

As she grew older, her career dreams came into clearer focus: she would attend nursing school and then join the Navy. A strong tradition of military service inhabits Tangier, which islanders like to say had the highest percentage of its population serve during World War II of any community in the United States. According to the island's history museum, 139 men served and eight died out of a population of about 1,000.

Tangier also has a tradition of young women marrying early, and she unexpectedly pursued that path. At age 17, she fell in love with Jerry Pruitt, a waterman and boat-builder who was twice her age. In 1979, near the end of her 11th grade year, they were married.

"I tell Jerry I married him so I could quit school, and I wouldn't have to take chemistry," she said with a laugh.

The courtship and marriage were a surprise to everyone, including herself, a teen who enjoyed music, reading and water skiing. She worked at a local sandwich shop and took four years of piano lessons. She described herself as an average student in school.

"I was not a bully," she said, "but I did not take anyone's crap. I grew up under two siblings who were eight and four years older than me and would dare me to do stuff. I would do it just to prove I was not scared of anything or anyone."

Classmates had been going steady with one another for years, but she wasn't among them. She really hadn't even had a boyfriend before falling for Pruitt.

"I was the least likely in my class to get married," she said, "and I was one of the first ones who got married."

It was shortly after she was married that she first met Dr. David Nichols in 1979, a month after he began coming to the island on a weekly basis. She made an appointment to see him because she was experiencing side effects from her birth-control medication. She told him she wanted him to write her a new prescription.

Not a chance, he said, without a physical examination. She explained she'd undergone a physical earlier that year before her wedding. His reply? He hadn't examined her, and he wouldn't write her a prescription until he had. It would prove to be the first of Pruitt's many encounters with Nichols' thoroughness and stubbornness. She underwent another physical.

Inez Pruitt. *Bob Brown/ Richmond Times-Dispatch.*

But there was something she liked about Nichols, and she trusted him right away. She started going to him on a regular basis, and he helped see her through two difficult pregnancies. She never bothered with finding pediatricians on the mainland for her daughters, Anna and Irene. She took them to Nichols.

He was straightforward and could "definitely get his point across," she recalled. As a patient, she had watched him stand his ground in an animated office conversation with his staff. The issue has been long forgotten, but not her original impression. "I remember thinking," she said, "he would be really hard to work for."

Pruitt wasn't looking for a job. Her work career included a summer at her husband's boatyard, where she learned to strike water lines and operate the lift used to raise boats from the water for maintenance. There also had been a stint working part-time as a chair-side assistant, receptionist and bill collector for a dentist who came to the island on a regular basis. Later, she opened a gift shop to make college money for her girls. But mostly in those years after high school she was a stay-at-home mom, raising her daughters, the job she loved most.

She never forgot her schooling, though. She came to regret not graduating from high school, so when her children were still young, she and her mother, who also had quit school at age 17 to get married, traveled east across the bay to the Eastern Shore to earn their GEDs. On the second day of testing, Pruitt grew homesick and discouraged and nearly walked away.

"But I sat back down and said, 'You've quit once, you're not going to quit a second time,'" she said. "I finished it, and I was very proud of myself for doing it. It wasn't easy, but I passed it."

Her older sister, Christy, a social worker, had taken a job with Nichols, handling paperwork for Medicaid, the federal health program for low-income Americans that some islanders were eligible to receive. On a Thursday in December 1987 Christy was away from the island, and Pruitt received a phone call from Nichols' nurse at the time, Beth Somers. They were slammed with patients, Somers said, and with Christy gone they were short-handed. Might Pruitt have time to pick up their lunches at Lorraine's, the island sandwich shop? Sure, Pruitt said. When she dropped off the sandwiches, Pruitt casually mentioned to Somers she was glad to help. Call on her anytime.

"Anytime" came sooner than Pruitt expected. Later that evening, Somers called again. Somers told her she and Nichols had been talking, and they wanted to know if Pruitt would be interested in coming to work at the clinic. Pruitt was intrigued, although she was a little uncertain what she had to offer. An interview was scheduled for the next Thursday that Nichols would be on the island: Christmas Eve.

'You work on Christmas Eve?" Pruitt asked incredulously. Somers' reply: Of course. The only Thursday Nichols or his associates never scheduled appointments on the island – except for when Christmas or New Year's Day fell on a Thursday – was Thanksgiving.

"I'll never forget it as long as I live," she said of that Christmas Eve interview in an exam room of the old clinic. "He just sat me down [and said]: This is what we do. This is what we'll require you to do. We'll require more stuff as you learn it. We're going to let you start filing charts, whatever Beth needs you to do. Whatever you're willing to learn, we're willing to teach you."

Any questions? Pruitt asked no questions, but offered a statement: she wanted no part of collecting money from patients. She hated doing that for the dentist, and she'd been fussed at and cussed at more than she cared to remember. Nichols said she wouldn't have to do that.

But the one thing Pruitt *really* remembers about that interview was when Nichols started talking, passionately, about patient confidentiality.

"If at any time when you're employed here I hear of you talking outside of this practice about a patient's condition or anything," he said, "you're fired."

Pruitt was taken aback; she hadn't even taken the job, and she felt he'd already threatened to fire her.

"I thought, 'Do I want this job?'" she recalled with a laugh.

She did.

"When do I start?" she asked.

Now, he said.

On Tangier, Christmas Eve is celebrated as enthusiastically as Christmas itself, with family gatherings all over the island and even fireworks – more than on the Fourth of July – with festivities traditionally beginning during daylight. Pruitt missed most of her family events that day, working a job she didn't have when she woke up that morning.

When Pruitt finally got home that evening, she had a throbbing headache – and a new holiday tradition, a positive spin she was able to develop only years later. She didn't get home in time to finish making dinner, so her family went to her sister-in-law's house, and from that year on Christmas Eve dinners rotated between their homes.

"Bah humbug, huh?" Nichols said many years later – with a smile – when Pruitt reminded him of her first day. Then he explained why it was important he came to the island every Thursday, even Christmas Eve. "That's just how you build a rapport and build a relationship of trust and faith and predictability."

That first day, however, Pruitt wasn't sure who was building what. Somers showed her around the office – which keys opened which cabinets, that sort of thing – but Pruitt remained uncertain about what she was doing there.

"Beth," Pruitt asked, "exactly what am I supposed to do?"

The bottom line, Somers told her in a voice Nichols wouldn't hear, is that when the doctor asked her to perform a task she didn't know how to do – and that time would certainly arrive sooner rather than later – just look for her and she would help.

"Don't let him know you don't know," Pruitt recalled Somers telling her. "Just act like you do know, go on your merry way and come get me."

But once she had been shown how to do some job around the clinic, Nichols expected her to remember it. Nichols was all about the patients, and those who worked for him were expected to help him deliver the best care possible. That meant, for members of the staff, being good at their jobs and being fast learners. No excuses.

Pruitt joked years later to Nichols – and everyone else – about her decision to join his practice.

"I had such a good life, such an uncomplicated life," she would say with a laugh many years later, shaking her head.

True to their words, Nichols and Somers began teaching her the medical business, from the ground up. She learned to draw blood and perform electrocardiograms and just about everything else that came up and needed doing. She learned to make X-rays the old-fashioned way, using rinses, chemicals and dryers, and then to fix the X-ray machine when it broke down, which happened from time to time with the old piece of equipment.

"She was wonderful," recalled Somers. "She was a quick learner. We just had a ball."

Pruitt's falling-out with Nichols in 1998 put a temporary strain on their relationship. After her return to the clinic, they never discussed the months she was away or revisited the reasons why she left. The icy divide between Nichols and Pruitt eventually thawed, and things returned to the way they were before she left – except she began doing less lab work and resumed working with patients, which made her happy. She also re-enrolled in the Nichols' School of Hard Knocks. Meantime, Pruitt's daughter Anna, who had volunteered at the office as a teen and loved it, began attending nursing school on the mainland, a result of Nichols' encouragement and her mother's example.

"She inspired me," said Anna Pruitt-Parks, who later wound up becoming a full-time paramedic and serving on the island's town council. "From watching her work [at the clinic] while I was growing up, the way she let me and my sister go with her to pack somebody's tooth and work with the dentist, to letting us play in the exam room. We'd pretend like we were doctors and nurses, and I just loved 'Rescue 911' and medical shows growing up. I knew that was what I wanted to do."

When she'd come home from class, her mother would quiz her on what she'd learned. Anna could see how excited her mother was for her. She also could see how much her mother wanted to go back to school herself.

By this point, patients had seen Pruitt around the office so long they came to trust her the way they trust a physician and just assumed she could take care of their medical needs, even calling on her in emergencies. They overlooked or forgot or simply didn't realize she had no formal training beyond a single class in cardiopulmonary resuscitation.

"People thought just because I worked for Dr. Nichols and Dr. Newman that I knew … how to make them well," Pruitt said with a laugh years later. "I'm like, 'Really?'"

She wanted to learn more, and Nichols encouraged her, saying the island needed a long-term medical presence, particularly a native Tangierman.

"From the get-go, he saw something in me that I didn't know was there," Pruitt said. "The willingness to learn, the eagerness to learn. He saw potential in me that I didn't know I had. I just loved what I was doing, but I didn't pay attention to what it might hold for me in the future."

She enrolled in a class for emergency medical technicians and thought she would work toward becoming a paramedic and hope she might be hired full-time by the Tangier fire department so she could make a living. While in that class, she heard about something she had not considered: the University of Maryland Eastern Shore, the closest university to Tangier, was starting a physician assistant program. In medical hierarchy, physician assistants (PAs) are between nurses and physicians. PAs are healthcare professionals licensed to practice medicine with physician supervision – even if that supervision is long-distance. PAs may conduct physical examinations, diagnose and treat illnesses, order and interpret tests, assist in surgery and write prescriptions.

Nursing had always been Pruitt's ambition, but there were other nurses on the island. Did she really want to go to the trouble of attending college on the mainland with the goal of working at the Tangier clinic just once a week when the doctor was in? Financially, nursing no longer made sense to Pruitt. Besides, what Tangier really needed was someone who could practice medicine between visits by Nichols or any other mainland physician. The more she looked into the PA program, the more it seemed like something that would benefit her and the island. Her kids were almost grown; Anna had graduated from nursing school, and Irene, the youngest, was a senior in high school. She talked to her husband, who told her to go for it. She talked to Nichols, who told her, "It's the answer to a prayer. This is exactly what Tangier needs."

Still, Pruitt doubted herself. She was almost 40. What she was about to embark on was something she had never dreamed for herself. "I would never in a million years ever thought I'd be a PA," she said. "Never." She felt no certainty that she could pull it off. Nichols assured her she could, reminding her how eager she'd always been to learn, and how she had become an integral part of the practice; how she'd learned how to diagnose and treat and do everything that was necessary. In her own way, she was as single-minded and stubbornly determined as he. She might have doubts, Nichols said, but he had none. Do it, he told her.

So, in 2001, Inez Pruitt, extremely anxious and slightly daunted, enrolled in college, and this was no roll-out-of-your-dorm-room-go-to-class-and-join-a-sorority college experience. It's difficult to overstate how challenging college can be for a wife and mother living on an island in the Chesapeake Bay who was more than two decades removed from high school. Early on, she arranged her class schedule so she could attend school on days the island's early-morning grocery boat made its supply runs to Crisfield. She caught the boat at 5:30 a.m., bouncing across occasionally rough seas for more than an hour, and drove the 20 miles to campus to be in class by 8 a.m. with students half her age. She would finish those exceedingly long, draining days by returning to Tangier in the evenings. In later years she needed to be on campus five days a week, meaning she had to give up working in the Tangier clinic, which distressed her and Nichols. She had to remain on the mainland, staying in a motel or sharing a room with the college-age daughter of a friend – an impossibly difficult transition for someone who had always lived within the comfortable embrace of Tangier and never, ever wanted to live anywhere else.

"There were many times she was ready to quit," Anna Pruitt-Parks said of her mother. "Many tears along the way. We just kept telling her – like she told me when I was having a hard time in nursing school – 'You've just got to get it done.' If she gets something in her head, she won't let go until it gets done."

In many ways, the logistics were more painful than the academics. She discovered in some of the medical-specific classes she seemed to have more knowledge than the other students and occasionally more experience than the instructors.

"Going to PA school was nothing," Pruitt said with a laugh. "I'd gone to the Nichols School of Hard Knocks."

For a test, the students were instructed to write a "SOAP" note – a medical evaluation physicians use that derives its name from the format it follows: **S**ubjective, **O**bjective, **A**ssessment and **P**lan. In her work at the Tangier clinic, Pruitt had read SOAP notes for years. She scored 110, earning extra credit, while many of the other students struggled to pass.

In 2007, after six years of classes and off-site clinical rotations, of overcoming doubts and chasing a dream she was surprised to learn she even had, Pruitt graduated and made history, at least in Nichols' estimation, who described her as "the first licensed practitioner of medicine in 400 years of history on this island."

In the process, she also had become something else.

Homer.

At first, Pruitt couldn't figure out why Nichols began calling her Homer. "I thought, 'I'm sure there's a compliment in there somewhere," she recalled with a laugh. There was.

"Homer" was Homer Wells, a character in John Irving's "The Cider House Rules." Nichols was immediately charmed by the 1999 movie, seeing a lot of Pruitt in Homer and a lot of himself in another character in the movie based on the 1985 novel, Dr. Wilbur Larch. He introduced Pruitt to the movie, and they took to calling each other Homer and Wilbur – like schoolyard nicknames – and wearing personalized white lab coats stitched with "Wilbur" and "Homer." Though the story has no connection to Tangier, the characters and their relationship bear an unmistakable resemblance to Pruitt and Nichols and theirs – except, of course, Homer was male.

Wilbur was the physician and founder of a fictitious orphanage in rural Maine in the early 1900s, having gone there to help those who needed it most. Homer, one of the abandoned children, was adopted and rejected by multiple families and kept coming back to the orphanage, where he grew to adulthood. Wilbur took Homer under his wing, raised him like a son, taught him the medical trade like an apprentice. Wilbur saw something in Homer, expected much of him and always instructed him to be "of some use."

Wilbur trained Homer in the ways of doctoring and surgery, and perhaps most critically, caring for the children who had no one else. Wilbur came to depend on Homer, down to the weekly showing of the orphanage's only movie, "King Kong," which invariably was interrupted when the film broke.

"Homer, I need you," Wilbur would say, calling on Homer for repairs.

Though Homer had no formal education, he could do everything a physician could. He was competent, reliable and humble. Wilbur envisioned Homer as his successor as the orphanage's physician, the perfect candidate to carry on the family business. Homer wanted to see the world. Or at least, the ocean.

So, Homer left the orphanage, much to Wilbur's dismay, and set off on an exploration during which he discovered something about the world and much about himself. He spurned letters from Wilbur, beckoning him back to the orphanage. Wilbur was forever telling Homer he was a doctor; Homer resisted, insisting he wasn't. It wasn't until the end, when he received a letter reporting the death of Wilbur, that Homer decided he must go home. When he got there, he was welcomed as a returning, well-loved hero, the person the orphanage needed most. He picked up where Wilbur left off, down to the nighttime ritual of bedtime stories and Wilbur's parting words when the lights were shut off: *"Good night you princes of Maine, you kings of New England."*

"Don't you love that line?" Nichols said to Pruitt

one day in the clinic when they were talking about the other Wilbur and Homer. "I love that movie."

Of course, the circumstances of their relationship were entirely different, and Pruitt never wanted to leave home. But the heart of the story is there: the mentoring, the respect, the disagreements, the stubbornness, the love. On a number of levels, "The Cider House Rules" is a story of being needed and the gift of accepting the call. Not unlike the story of Nichols and Pruitt. In the movie, what Wilbur started, Homer continued. On Tangier, Nichols had positioned Pruitt to do the same.

Said islander Norma Dize, "She's so good because he trained her. A lady Dr. Nichols. She takes just as much interest in us. Of course, she's really one of us."

The nameplates outside their offices in the Taniger health center reflected the nicknames Nichols and Pruitt had adopted from characters in the book and film, "The Cider House Rules." Pruitt was Homer, and Nichols was Wilbur.
Bill Lohmann

Nichols greets patient and friend Alice Pruitt on a visit to Tangier in August 2010.
Bob Brown/Richmond Times-Dispatch.

NINE

SAVING LIVES, MAKING FRIENDS
*'You saved up your aches and pains
until Thursday'*

When you live in a lovely, though isolated, place like Tangier, you develop an acute appreciation for things many of us on the mainland take for granted – such as convenient access to everything, including medical care. You fully understand, particularly if your family has been there for generations, that part of the tradeoff of living on a small island is there will not always be a doctor just down the lane, that the nearest hospitals and physicians offering specialized care are a boat ride away and that the effort in trying to reach them might evolve into something more akin to an ordeal.

Leaving the island for medical care is something Norma Dize, from an early age, was all too familiar with. As a young child, she was diagnosed with polio and sent to Richmond for four months of treatment at what, in the 1930s, was then called Crippled Children's Hospital. As the seagull flies, the distance between Richmond and Tangier is about 80 miles. By a combination of boat and car or truck, it takes about four hours. To a 7-year-old child who had never been away from the island or her family, Richmond might as well have been on the other side of the world. Homesickness became her secondary diagnosis.

"Mama had an uncle who lived in Urbanna (on Virginia's Middle Peninsula), and we went over to the Western Shore, and he took us down there," Dize said. "Mama had to leave me, so I had neither my mama or daddy to visit me. I screamed and cried, but I had a doctor and a nurse who both took to me. They were so good to me. They kept me in penny postcards to write Mama."

In her 80s, Dize sat in the living room of the island home where she and husband Pres (short for Preston) had lived for almost 60 years, just a few paces from the house where she grew up. Her sisters lived in adjacent houses; their father had bought the property and carved it up among the children. She and Pres raised three daughters and had been married for 66 years, at the time of the 2010 interview. All in all, a wonderful life, she said, although not without a few bumps along the way, which still occur from time to time. A waterman, Pres was just getting over a broken collarbone he suffered when he fell off a dock at a crab shanty. He was 84 at the time of the fall.

"Worst hurt I ever had in my life," said Pres, a friendly man of few words who let his wife do most of the talking. He was taken to a hospital on the Maryland shore for treatment: by boat, 45 minutes dock-to-dock. With a broken collarbone.

"Tough" is an applicable adjective for Tangiermen, but they have their limits.

"I hated spinach with a passion," Norma Dize recalled of her stay at the hospital in Richmond. "We had a cook down there. Her name was Gertie; I guess it was Gertrude, but everybody called her Gertie. She sort of took to me. I don't know if she knew I didn't have any family to see me. But I hated spinach. You know the garbage cans you put your toe on and open the lid? I can see her now, looking all around and she'd open it and scoop [my spinach] in the garbage can. I don't guess that would have been protocol.

"Then we had to drink two glasses of milk every meal. The first glass, we had to take a tablespoon of cod liver oil and put our spoon down in it and drink that milk with the yellow floating on it. I'd get sick on my stomach. And she'd throw it down the sink. She did that for me."

Later that year, when Dize returned to Richmond for a checkup, she and her mother were walking along a downtown street when she spied a familiar face.

"Gertie!" Dize yelled, pulling away from her mother who didn't quite know what to think, and running to meet her old friend. "She grabbed me, and we hugged each other. She had been so good to me. She was my friend."

Which is exactly how, many decades later, she came to think of David Nichols.

"I've had a good life, and Dr. Nichols has been such a part of it – such a part," she said. "Just a wonderful doctor. Friend. I got so I loved him so well. No crush or anything, but you know how you love your doctor. And I know he loves us. You can tell when somebody's sincere. You surely can."

She nodded toward her husband. "He's sitting here because of Dr. Nichols."

After Pres experienced chest pains while on a walk six years earlier, Nichols insisted he go to the mainland immediately for further tests. The Dizes followed his advice. Turned out Pres had "a 99 percent blockage and was in for a major heart attack," Norma recalled. Pres underwent heart bypass surgery, and that crisis was avoided.

"He was the greatest diagnostician I have ever talked to in my life," Norma Dize said. "My daughter lives in Washington, and she said, 'If I ever get something wrong with me and I don't know what it is, he's who I'm going to.'

"You saved up your aches and pains until Thursday when he was coming," she said with a laugh. "You'd wait for him. That's the truth."

Nichols loved talking to patients. He considered it a critical part of any appointment, but he also thought it important to make it a conversation and not an interrogation. So after entering the examination room he would sit because he wanted to speak to patients at eye-level, not while towering above them. He never wanted the patients to think he was talking down to them.

"He wanted to let patients know he had all the time in the world," said his daughter Sarah.

"You'd thought he never had another care in the world," said Kim Clark, his long-time assistant in White Stone. "If there was something on your mind, he'd always pull it out of you. He'd always say, 'Is there anything else I can do for you?'"

Nichols would often ask his patients to rate how they were feeling on a scale of 1-to-10, with 10 being best. If the response was "10," Nichols would reply, "Well, what would it take to make it 11?"

"And he would listen," recalled his brother Peter Nichols. "And he would do anything he could as a doctor and a friend to make that happen. I hope I'm wrong, but I think David was one of the last of the true country doctors. I don't think there are going to be many more like David."

Nichols proudly considered himself a "country doctor," not only from the perspective of living and practicing away from big cities, but from the very approach of ultra-personalized care that is suggested by the notion of country medicine: a familiar, holistic and kindly approach to a patient's needs. In contrast, he hated the concept of "corporate medicine," where the emphasis is on efficiency and physicians are rewarded for seeing more patients in less time.

"Some people would argue that if you're seeing more people, taking care of more of their problems faster, then you're doing a better job than when you saw fewer people and spent more time with them," he said during an interview in 2010. "I just know you can't do a patient justice by rushing them through the door. You have to spend time with them. The one thing technology can't replace is your one-on-one relationship with the patient, the rapport you have with them. I feel so comfortable that I can go into a room with a patient … and listen to their problems, just sit there and make them feel at ease. I feel so totally comfortable that I can do that, and I can make them walk out of that office feeling better."

"I know there's got to be change, but where is the boundary? There's not enough commitment these days. Part of it is the young docs don't want to give up their whole life for medical care, and I can't fault them for that. But don't cheapen medicine in the process of doing that."

Anita Crockett picked up her 4-month-old daughter Stephanie Paige Crockett and held her, but something didn't feel quite right. The baby's back felt cold. Crockett thought it might be pneumonia, so she took the baby to Nichols, who examined her not just for pneumonia but for something more. He put his stethoscope to her chest and her back and listened intently. He wasn't sure what he was hearing, but it didn't sound right. The chatter from down the hall drifted into the exam room and distracted him, so he took Stephanie Paige into the back of the clinic, put her on the X-ray table and shut the door.

"I want total quiet!" he said to everyone else in the clinic. Then he listened some more.

Finally, he said, "I hear it. I hear it." What he heard was a faint sound between the baby's heartbeat: a murmur.

"We had no clue," Crockett said. "We got blown away. He said it was a hole in her heart."

Stephanie Paige needed to see a specialist right away, Nichols said. He wouldn't even let Crockett wait until the next day. He insisted Crockett and her husband, Clint, hire a boat immediately and travel to the mainland.

Doctors there put the baby on medication and performed surgery a few months later when she was stronger and repaired two holes in her heart.

"If it hadn't been for him," Crockett said, "she'd have been a goner."

When Stephanie Paige was 3 years old, she also had hernia surgery.

"He found that, too," she said. "It was a good feeling to know he'd be coming in every Thursday, no matter what."

Over the years, Nichols developed a well-earned reputation as a first-rate diagnostician who was not reluctant about running as many tests as he saw necessary to get to the bottom of whatever issue a patient was experiencing.

Inez Pruitt once said to Nichols, "Everything I do in this practice and practice in general I have to answer to you. Who do you have to answer to?" His quick reply: "I answer to the patients."

"A brilliant doctor," said Dewey Crockett, the preacher, teacher and former mayor who also worked as a trained volunteer in the island's clinic during summers. "He could diagnose even with the [old] equipment we had. We were limited, but he could diagnose cases, and usually when you went to a hospital to a specialist, he'd hit it right on the head. He was really that good."

Crockett echoed what a lot of Tangiermen said about Nichols: "We would have lost a lot of people … if he hadn't been coming so faithful. He detected their problems before it got out of hand." Crockett was convinced of this in a very personal way.

"Oh, my," he said, "I'd have been dead a long time ago if it hadn't been for him."

Crockett had myriad health problems: heart, kidneys, hip. The worst came on a stormy spring evening in 2009 when Crockett was sitting in his living room with his wife and son watching "Wheel of Fortune!"

"My head just went over to the side. I never felt shortness of breath, never felt pain," Crockett said. "My wife told my son to call 911. They both got me out of the chair and onto the floor and started CPR. Inez and Anna came. Then all the [ambulance] squad. They had [Nichols, who was on the mainland] on the phone talking to him while Inez and all of them were working on me."

Using mouth-to-mouth resuscitation and electric shock, Pruitt and the others managed to restore Crockett's heartbeat, but his ordeal was far from over. He needed to get to a hospital quickly, but the bad weather that evening and the lack of available transportation left him stranded on the island, at least temporarily, far from a hospital and fighting for his life. Finally, a Virginia State Police helicopter in suburban Richmond became available, and it arrived to airlift him off the island and carry him to VCU Medical Center in Richmond, where he underwent heart-bypass surgery.

That's the high medical drama of living on a tiny island, but sometimes the day-to-day business of doctoring in such an out-of-the-way place was, if not so dramatic, equally as demanding – and fulfilling.

"One day in the summer when I was working with him we had three emergencies at the same time: a guy in there with a heart problem, a baby and a lady tourist who had fallen and broken her ankle," Crockett recalled. "We were taking care of all of them, and [Nichols] came out in the hallway lit up like a Christmas tree and looked at me and said, 'Dewey, this is what I call practicing medicine!'"

"I can tell you," said Kim Clark, who worked with Nichols longer than anyone, "David Nichols, from day one, 100 percent cared about his patients. That's why he was so detail-oriented, why he expected perfection [from his staff]. I always admired him for the care and devotion he gave his patients.

"In 31 years, it was rare we didn't go to Tangier [each week]. Even when the weather was so bad people couldn't get out of their houses [on the island], he'd still go. His saying was, 'I made a commitment to these people, and they learned to trust me, and we've got to show up.' You're not just talking about flying to Tangier for 31 years. You're talking about spending the entire day, coming back mentally and physically exhausted and still having work to do when he got back [in White Stone]. That's commitment."

Added Clark, "I don't think people realize how much Tangier meant to him."

Routine medical procedures are complicated when the patient lives on an island. Consider colonoscopies. The day-before prep work required of a patient makes taking a ferry to the mainland the morning of the procedure problematic. Would you want to be on a boat in the middle of the Chesapeake Bay in that condition? The only alternative was going over to the mainland the day before and spending the night in a hotel – and it didn't promise to be a pleasant stay. So when Nichols began performing colonoscopies on Tangier, it was a godsend for patients – not to mention the boat captains who no longer had to ferry these patients to their appointments.

One morning, a Tangierman dutifully showed up for his colonoscopy at the clinic. He was fully prepared, you might say, and ready to go. Nichols was about to begin the procedure when he discovered an unexpected problem: the light bulb on the colonoscopy equipment was burned out. A search of the clinic turned up no replacement bulbs. Send the patient home and have him come back another day? Nope. Nichols climbed back in his helicopter, flew back to his White Stone office, picked up a new bulb and a few to spare, re-fueled, and flew back to Tangier, replaced the bulb and performed the colonoscopy.

"Now," Nichols said years later, "I have extra bulbs."

When she was 17, Virginia "Ginny" Marshall was on her father's boat when the motor was fired up and the engine's exhaust blew sooty debris all over her. It made a mess of her white skirt and tan-and-white blouse, but something far worse happened: a tiny piece of coal went into her eye.

"Before we got home, I couldn't see," she recalled. She went to Johns Hopkins Hospital in Baltimore where doctors examined her day after day and performed test after test, some involving needles inserted into her eye, trying to determine what could be done to restore her sight. She traveled to Pittsburgh where she had relatives, and a doctor there gave her the bad news: the hot piece of coal had burned the tissue in her eye. Her vision was gone in that eye, which was later removed. She came home to Tangier with only one working eye. More than 70 years later, she was philosophical about her misfortune.

"That's life, isn't it?" she said.

She came to appreciate a physician like Nichols who would "sit down and talk to you," she said.

"You go to a doctor now, you're in and out so quick, you don't know what you have or what you don't have," Marshall said. "Dr. Nichols took time with you."

She also valued how quickly he became part of the community and earned the trust of his new patients, no small achievement in a place that can be difficult for an outsider to enter.

"I think he fit in as soon as he got here," she said.

An older woman on the island had undergone open-heart surgery but was feeling poorly after she returned home, Inez Pruitt recalled.

"I called Dr. Nichols, and he said to send her to the hospital," Pruitt said. "But she insisted I call the surgeon who said … 'Give it a day to get over it.'"

The woman chose to follow the surgeon's advice and stayed home. The next day, she was worse. It wasn't a Thursday, but Nichols flew to Tangier, went to her home, helped get her to the clinic and diagnosed her with heart block. Nichols arranged for her to fly immediately to the mainland for treatment. Nichols' son, Davy, was a teen at the time, and he rode with the woman in the island's ambulance to the airfield.

"She took Davy's hand," Pruitt recalled, "and she said, 'Davy, I love your dad as if he were my own son.'"

A patient arrived with shortness of breath, and a severe heart arrhythmia was diagnosed. Nichols believed the man needed immediate treatment in the form of a brief electric shock to reset his heart rhythm to its normal pattern. Nichols provided the instructions, and the nurse on duty applied the shock once. Then a second time.

The patient survived, but was not thrilled at the shocking experience.

"He raised up and said, 'Goddamn, you killed me!'" Inez Pruitt recalled with a laugh.

"And," Nichols said, driving home the point, "Tangier people never say bad words. I don't think he was real anxious to see me a lot afterwards."

Nichols had his own shocking experience, albeit inadvertently as he attempted to repair an X-ray table. As a frugal businessman, he was a big proponent of saving the cost of bringing service technicians to the island, so he was always encouraging his staff to learn to repair broken-down equipment. On the X-ray table, an electrical wire had malfunctioned, and Nichols decided he would attempt to fix the problem with a paperclip.

"I said, 'Let me turn off the power first,'" Inez Pruitt recalled. Apparently she didn't offer fast enough, and Nichols got the shock of his life. "It threw him clear against the wall," Pruitt said.

"It did?" replied Nichols, listening to the story years later. "Are you sure? Why don't I remember it?"

"Because you got shocked!" Pruitt said, still laughing. "I told him he's no electrician, so he should keep his day job."

Aside from injuries sustained while pretending to be a tradesman, Nichols played hurt on a number of occasions on Tangier. He arrived – and worked – with broken fingers and at least once with a bum toe that he'd dropped an iron on and had to ask a medical student who came along to drain the resulting subungual hematoma.

"I dropped the iron on my toe trying to iron my pants in the morning," Nichols explained. "I didn't iron very well."

Another episode involving Nichols and the X-ray room wasn't quite so funny. Pruitt had noticed he had been more quiet than usual, and then he asked her into the X-ray room for a quick consultation. She thought she might be about to get reprimanded for something, though she didn't know what. Instead, Nichols said he needed to take a kidney X-ray.

"Which patient?" she asked.

"Me," he said.

He told her he was passing a kidney stone. She wondered why he had come to Tangier and not remained at home, passing a kidney stone being the sort of painful unpleasantness one would seemingly prefer to experience outside of the workplace.

He wondered where the kidney stone was.

Pruitt handed him a gown.

"What's this for?" he asked.

"You've got to take your pants off," she replied.

He balked. "'You take the clothes off everybody who comes in this door," Pruitt said.

"I'm not taking my pants off," he said.

"I'm not taking your X-ray," she said.

Pruitt won. Sort of. Nichols got on the X-ray table, screened by a drape. The stone eventually passed.

Like many of Nichols' patients on Tangier, Marian Pruitt was devout in her faith. Unlike most of the others, though, she always would bring inspirational reading material from a religious column she had clipped from a newspaper to her appointments.

"She lived to be in her 90s," Nichols said, "and she was a firm believer of such strong faith. Every time I'd see her, she'd pull out that little piece of paper and sit me down and read it and go through it with me. Every time I saw her."

It got so when her appointment was over, Nichols would gather the staff and have them hear the reading, too.

'He'd get us all together and say, 'OK, sit down, I want you to listen,'" Inez Pruitt recalled. "At first I thought he was being a little smart, but he wasn't. He was serious."

Nichols was serious. He was quite taken with the spirituality of Tangiermen, believing the island "has got to be one of the most Christian communities in the world. When you come here you're just surrounded by it. They practice it in their lives. They are more interested in human connectedness than they are in materialism. What surprises me more than anything is a lot of the people go on missions. They fly to India, they fly to Louisiana. They go all over the place, and they are not well-to-do-people. I think their religion drives their life, and I think it's great."

Practicing medicine on an island – without easy access to everything – requires occasional improvisation.

A patient with a rapid heart rhythm came into the office, and Nichols asked Pruitt if she had any balloons handy. What? Balloons, he said. Like for a birthday party? The office was really hopping that day – the only empty space for this patient was the clinic's dental room – and Inez Pruitt had no clue why, in the middle of all this bedlam, Nichols was asking for balloons. But she dutifully went to a nearby gift shop and purchased a package of balloons and brought them back to the clinic. Nichols handed one to the patient and asked her to try to blow it up. The woman began puffing into the balloon, and soon her heart rate was back to normal.

"Every time he was here," Pruitt said, "it was something new."

Burke and Bonnie Landon came to consider Nichols family. "Like a brother," Burke said.

"He's our angel," Bonnie said.

Nichols tended to the medical needs of the Landons as well as Bryan, their grown son who has autism. "When he came here, Bryan was only 7 or 8 years old, and right away he took to Dr. Nichols," Bonnie said. "He's so likeable."

She also recalled that her mother had been a patient of Nichols. "She liked him so well. On one of her visits she said to him, 'Dr. Nichols, you're sweet as sugar!' Not long ago, that's what he said to me. He said, 'Your mom used to say it to me, and now I'm going to say it to you!'"

Burke is a sturdy, gregarious man who made his living on the water for more than a half-century. Once he arrived in his 70s, he made concessions to age, giving up oystering in the winter ("a young man's job," he said) but continued to crab, loving the work and the water too much to quit. "I'm going to go as long as I can get aboard the boat," he said.

Burke is the sort of man you could imagine not noticing that he was sick. A few years earlier, he had undergone tests at the clinic. When the results returned, showing Burke had suffered a slight heart attack but was susceptible to another, Nichols and Pruitt made a beeline for the Landon home.

"I was sitting down ready to get a good pot of Jimmy [male blue] crabs, and they come over and say, 'You're going to the helicopter,'" Burke recalled. "I said, 'No, we've got a pot of Jimmies, and I'm going to eat my crabs first. 'No, you're not, you're going,' they said.

"I didn't get my Jimmies," Burke said with a laugh. He boarded the helicopter and was flown to a mainland hospital where doctors put in a heart stent.

Bonnie had her own stories: Nichols had diagnosed her diabetes, treated her high blood pressure and helped her navigate through the uncertainty, the anxiety and the insurance coverage of knee replacement surgery, which, she said, changed her life.

"I got it done, and I thank him," she said. "I've been a new person since I got them."

Said Bonnie of Nichols, "He's dear to our hearts."

With arthritic knees and in her 80s, Jean Parks Autry always stopped by the clinic a few weeks before Christmas to get a steroid injection – so she would feel good enough to go Christmas shopping in Maryland.

"I keep hurting," she said with a laugh, "until I have to go shopping."

Autry visited a physician in Salisbury before Nichols came to Tangier. Then she stayed home for her medical needs. Nichols also tended to her parents. At age 90, her father developed a melanoma on his nose, and Nichols made a house-call to remove it. When Nichols was done, Autry's father looked at the physician and said, "Dr. Nichols, you know what I'd have done today if I'd known you were coming?"

"What, Mr. Parks?"

"I'd have gone to Chicago."

Everyone had a good laugh.

"He was so caring and understanding," Autry said of Nichols. "He'd hug on you when you got ready to leave. I guess that's what made him so special."

Another year just before Christmas, Nichols was getting ready to leave the island one Thursday evening after a full day at the clinic. On his way through the gate he was met by Betty McMann, who used to work in the clinic and was a longtime patient. McMann had fallen off a ladder while decorating the church for Christmas, and was holding her arm awkwardly close to her body.

"You always know it's broken when they cradle it like a baby," Pruitt said.

Nichols stayed, of course, and treated McMann's arm and put her in a cast. He was a little later getting home, but that wasn't unusual. He would do pretty much anything for anyone on Tangier, particularly McMann. She had come to work with him years earlier as a receptionist and eventually became a nursing assistant. "I'm not going to stick anybody," she told him, "but I'll do any other job you want me to do."

Because she was older, McMann said she was treated less like an employee and "more like a mom. He would put up with more from me than he would from anyone else." If he said an overly sharp word to someone, McMann responded with a "Dr. Nichols!" that would serve as a motherly reprimand and get his attention. "Once in a while he could bite," she said, "but he was mostly all bark." Hers was the first voice he would hear when he called the clinic to report he was running late and stuck at the drawbridge on the mainland, trying to reach the airport.

When her brother-in-law was diagnosed with cancer, Nichols took McMann into a room at the clinic and broke the news. "He let me cry on his shoulder," she said.

When she developed lymphoma, she underwent aggressive chemotherapy and lost her hair – "Seventy-seven years old," she said, "and I was bald-headed" – and Nichols came to visit her. "When I sat up to greet him, he said, 'Beautiful, beautiful!'" McMann recalled, "and I cried."

"A gem," McMann said of Nichols.

Despite antibiotics and time, Denny Crockett couldn't seem to shake a case of double-pneumonia. It seemed like he was better, but something wasn't quite right. Blood tests showed Crockett's disease-fighting white blood cells were still high. When Nichols couldn't figure out what the cells were fighting, he sent Crockett to a mainland specialist and ordered an X-ray and scan. The physician made the X-ray but not a scan, didn't see anything and sent him home. Nichols was furious. He sent Crockett the next day and demanded a scan – which showed a tumor in one of his kidneys.

Crockett had returned home before learning the results of the scan. It was Pruitt's weekend duty at the White Stone office – she worked in Nichols' mainland office on occasion – when she and Nichols got a look at the results on a Saturday. As they studied the report, they shed tears, Pruitt said. Nichols was planning to fly Pruitt back to Tangier anyway, but he insisted on accompanying her to Crockett's home to break the news. Pruitt called and let Crockett know she would be coming. She didn't

mention Nichols would be there, too, but he noticed omi-
nously that he never heard Nichols' helicopter take off
again after it landed with Pruitt.

"If he comes, too," Crockett thought to himself,
"this is not good news."

Crockett, in his 50s, was retired principal of the
island's school. He now operates Tangier Oil Co., and
with his wife, Glenna, owns Hilda Crockett's Chesapeake
House restaurant and bed-and-breakfast. Pruitt had been
in Crockett's high school history class years before.

Nichols and Pruitt told him about the cancer and
their plans to send him to a specialist that Monday and
start attacking the disease.

"He was gentle like he is," Crockett said about the
conversation. "He said, 'Denny, I don't know what the
future is going to hold, but the doctor I'm sending you to
can tell you.'"

Because it was caught early, the cancer was con-
tained, and the tumor was extracted laparoscopically.
Crockett never felt anything that would have led him
to believe he had kidney problems, likely because his
good kidney increased its function to cover for the fail-
ing kidney. The surgeon told him it was good the tumor
was removed when it was. It was on the verge of growing
more aggressive, the surgeon said.

"I'd have been a goner if not for this bunch," Crockett said of the staff at the island clinic. "Dr. Nichols saved my life. He's a gentleman the whole time he's working with you, but he's just like a bulldog. He won't give up once he gets ahold of something. If something's wrong, he won't give up until he finds out what's going on."

Crockett also appreciated that in his doggedness, Nichols didn't try to be a hero with someone else's health. Nichols gladly acknowledged when cases moved beyond his expertise and would seek help from specialists. Some might view that as a sign of weakness. Patients like Crockett saw it as an enviable – and life-saving – trait.

"That's the kind of doctor I want," Crockett said. "Some doctors don't want you to get a second opinion because that seems like it's stepping on their toes. With life and death, you don't worry about toes."

Bob Newman has numerous stories of his own from alternating with Nichols every other Thursday on Tangier. One that stands out is of the Tangierman who was cleaning under his dock when he was poked through a hand with the barbed spine of a stingray.

"He came in with this thing stuck in his hand," Newman recalled. "Sort of a dramatic thing. He was actually pretty calm about it. Fortunately, I'd done a fair amount of ER [emergency room] work. We just numbed his hand and took the thing out. The tendon wasn't involved, so it was actually a pretty simple thing.

"But it was the sort of thing you'd never see on the mainland."

Like Nichols, Newman also saw his share of visitors in need of medical care – like the traveler who came in a sailboat, stayed the night on the island and was preparing to shove off when he cut his wrist deeply on a metal clip on one of the sails.

"He had a radial artery laceration, and he was bleeding heavily," Newman said. "He came in with multiple towels soaked with blood. We controlled that with pressure, called the helicopter and got him over to a vascular surgeon [on the mainland]."

As great as the need was for medical care on Tangier and as much as Nichols felt drawn to be there, his medical practice on the island was never a profitable venture, he said. "I wasn't making any money here, although the people in town didn't think that," Nichols said with a laugh in a 2010 interview. "They thought I was walking home with a briefcase full of money."

In 2009, for example, the expenses related to the Tangier part of his practice exceeded revenues by $100,000, Nichols said, and he even showed his books to Ooker Eskridge, the mayor, just in case anyone doubted the financial realities of what he had been doing for so many years. The time of a staff member or two and the cost of flying them to the island every week – even though he was able to work out an arrangement with Medicare to receive partial reimbursement for his plane expenses – was a costly proposition. Patients were not charged a "transportation fee," as some on the island thought. Nichols absorbed whatever flight expenses were not covered by Medicare.

"The White Stone practice subsidized Tangier all those years," Nichols said. "If it weren't for a bustling practice in White Stone, I couldn't afford to come out [to Tangier]. But the bottom line was not to make a profit [on Tangier], but just to help out."

It didn't help that perhaps 50 percent of patients on the island did not have health insurance, he said, and many of those could not afford to fully pay for their medical care. Nichols understood that and often let patients run tabs for long periods of time, and just as often, forgave considerable sums that families owed the practice, explaining "if you ain't got it, you ain't got it." Plus, he said, "If someone was having difficulty and couldn't do it, I'd just forget it. We were doing it for more than money."

Although, he acknowledged, there were times he felt some patients "abused" his relaxed approach to bill-collecting and accumulated debts in the thousands of dollars without making an effort to repay any of it. For the most part, though, people paid what they could when they could.

"I had one lady pay $10 a month for five years to pay off her husband's debt," Nichols said. "She was doing the best she could. I also had people you would give discounts to. If they didn't have insurance, we would charge them less."

And patients often would bring him gifts: books, cards, homemade goodies from the kitchen.

"But the thing I get most is hugs and kisses," he said. "All the time. All these years. You don't go and see a patient without getting a hug first."

Nurse Tess Owens has a habit of rubbing a patient's arm or leg as a way to comfort them through procedures. On this particular day, a patient came in for a Pap smear.

"So I think I'm rubbing the patient's leg, but it turns out it's Dr. Nichols' arm I'm rubbing," she said, laughing at the recounting. "He looks over at me and says, 'What are you doing?' I said, 'I just want you calm through this procedure.' It was a riot. I'll never forget it."

Did Nichols see the humor in the episode? "Eventually," she said.

Nichols could be a little tense and testy, and his staff used to yank his chain from time to time. A favorite trick was opening blinds. He hated that. He wanted privacy for the patients and insisted they be shut tight. So naturally, on occasion, staff members would make certain the blinds were open just to get a rise out of him.

"I realize that's passive-aggressive," Owens said with a laugh. "But it worked for us."

She also had a habit of saying, "Oops!" whenever something went awry.

Nichols would say, "Tess, don't ever say, 'Oops!' in front of a patient."

On a breezy spring morning, Nichols phoned Inez Pruitt at home to inquire about the weather before flying over from White Stone. He noted it was a bit windy on the mainland. How hard was it blowing on the island? Pruitt handed the phone to her husband, Jerry, who had already been out that morning.

"Forty [mph], gusting to 50," Jerry Pruitt told him, easily enough to keep any sane pilot grounded. Nichols came anyway, though he traveled alone. No nurses wanted any part of flying that day. In fact, some patients on the island had called and said it was too windy for them to *walk* to the clinic.

"I was in the waiting room," said Inez Pruitt, "and [Nichols] walked in and said, 'That was some damn wind!'"

He measured it at 48 mph as he landed.

"I just wanted people to know I'd be here every Thursday," Nichols said.

An older patient, perhaps 90, arrived in the Tangier clinic with "an ugly-looking thing on her shin," recalled Nichols, who suspected a form of cancer. A wide incision would be required, and on a part of the leg where the skin is stretched tight over the bone Nichols didn't believe he was best equipped to handle it.

"This needs to be done by a plastic surgeon," he said. "You go to a hospital, doctors can do pathology."

The patient's reply: "Absolutely not. I'm not going, and you're doing it."

Nichols insisted again that she travel to the mainland for care. Again, she refused. The strong-willed patient was not unlike a lot of Tangier residents who wanted no part of going to the mainland for medical care for any number of reasons: they didn't like hospitals, they didn't want to spend the money or they didn't want to deal with people they didn't know.

"I'm going to die with it then," she said.

Nichols finally relented. OK, he said, "I can try."

Nichols and Pruitt numbed the area, cut off the growth, and – as Nichols and Pruitt grunted and groaned, and the patient gritted her teeth – sewed the tight skin back together. The pathology report indicated they had removed all of the cancer. When the patient returned the next week for a follow-up exam, she was nonchalant about it all.

"What's the big deal?" she said. "I told you."

Nichols was a burger man. Everyone who knew him knew it – on occasion much to their dismay.

Allan Riggs, the physician assistant who worked with Nichols in the early 1980s, recalled the time Nichols flew a Tangier resident to the mainland, and in gratitude she offered Nichols a cooler of fresh crabmeat.

"I was drooling with this cooler of crabmeat (nearby)," Riggs remembered, "and David said, 'I really don't like seafood. Just buy me a hamburger next time I'm over on Tangier.' I started to cry."

Deep down, Riggs knew he could have anticipated Nichols' response. When Riggs was working a few days with Nichols during his extended interview for the job, they finished their morning appointments early and didn't have another patient for a few hours, so Nichols suggested they fly to Newport News for lunch.

"I was thinking shrimp and crabmeat," Riggs said with a laugh. "Instead, we went to McDonald's."

Said his longtime assistant Clark, "That's his all-time favorite place: McDonald's. Can you believe it?"

Nichols served on a bank board, and he would call Clark say, "I finished my bank meeting. You want some McDonald's?"

For his birthday one year, his staff took Nichols to McDonald's for a party. Little kids party hats and all. He loved it.

Amid all of the faithfulness of mission that Nichols talked about and displayed through the years, there were times he grew frustrated and discouraged and could become as ruffled as anyone, said Inez Pruitt.

"This just isn't working," she heard him say on more than one occasion. "I've got to quit."

"I looked him straight in the eye and said, 'You couldn't quit if you tried.'" And she was right: he couldn't, so he didn't.

Though he did obstetrical work in his early days in White Stone, he never delivered a baby on Tangier. "Always wanted to," he said, "but never did."

However, he did just about everything else on the island. Nichols never had any idea of who or what would come through the door of the clinic every Thursday: tumors that needed draining, poison ivy, anything.

"One week, we had six or seven patients and there was heart failure, pancreatic cancer, MRSA skin infection," he said. "It was like a little ICU."

Bob Newman, Nichols' longtime associate in the White Stone practice, said some of the cases on Tangier were the sickest people they treated. In White Stone, the practice included wealthy retirees as well as poor and uninsured patients, but the majority of patients that came to the White Stone office were insured, Newman said.

"We had a fairly easy-to-manage practice," he said. "The Tangier days were always a challenge. The toughest days and the hardest days, but you just felt good about it. You felt you were doing good things for people."

Newman fell in love with Tangier just like Nichols did. And just like Nichols, it took a while for the people of Tangier to warm to a new face.

"I was there a few years before people would not see him and see me," said Newman, who for a time alternated Thursday trips to Tangier with Nichols, noting that some patients would delay office visits until Nichols returned to the island. Early on, when Tangier patients did seek out Newman for care it was "usually under a circumstance that they were sick and forced to see me," he said.

But after a few years of faithful visits, Newman became what he called "an accepted insider" on the island, and like Nichols, a trusted friend. He described Tangier as "the kind of place you want to practice medicine." A place, he said, where the work is needed and where the people, despite being wary of newcomers at first, are genuine and appreciative, and once they come around, as kind and generous and welcoming as anyone.

He described the notion of visiting and working on Tangier as "almost a fairy tale of a story when you think about it. Just that flight across the bay. It's just an unbelievable experience, to be up there in a small plane and know you're going to that small dot out in the water. I was always amazed at just the trip, and I contemplated life in general as we flew across."

As a result, his own "love affair with Tangier" developed over the 15 years he worked with Nichols.

"It was like going back 50 years in time," he said. "They've become much more modern now with satellite dishes, etc., but back then it was literally before the age of computers, before the connectedness of the Internet. It was very much different. Just a lovely place. The beauty of it is the simple values and the simplicity of life with very little focus on what your material possessions are. Just a fabulous place."

Newman left the White Stone practice in 2002 to go into academic family medicine, fulfilling his ambition to teach residents and students the principles of primary care. Before he departed,though, the people of Tangier threw him a going-away party at the island's school.

"One of my greatest memories" Newman said. "It was hard to leave, actually. They're just a loving people."

Nichols said Tangier shaped him as a physician.

"Just coming over to Tangier changed me," he said. "There are no quick visits here. They're complicated. Much more complicated than in White Stone. The other thing is, it taught me to sit down and take the time with patients. Really get into their history and not rush them. Delve into their past. After a while, you just want to sit and hear a story from a patient. Just talk to them."

Dewey Crockett saw the way Nichols treated patients, both as a patient and as a member of the clinic staff.

"If you were the last patient of the day and he had had 25 or 30 patients, and some days he did, he spent just as much time with you as he did with the first," Crockett said. "He was never in a hurry. He took his time. He was thorough.

"Every elderly patient, when he finished doing their medical exams, he'd put his arm around them – they just loved him dearly – and he'd just say, 'We'll get to the bottom of this,' and he would."

He also was honest and straightforward with his diagnoses, and he saw no purpose in sugar-coating bad news, said Inez Pruitt. He was matter-of-fact, not an alarmist, but he was truthful.

"He's not pretentious with his patients," she said. "He doesn't hold back if a patient wants to know. He's going to tell them what's going on. He's not mean at all, but he will be point-blank. He will be honest with them, and he will make sure they understand."

Christmas was generally a day off for Nichols, but even his patients were still on his mind. In fact, in what became a holiday tradition he would spend a chunk of time every Christmas morning phoning patients on Tangier and from his White Stone practice to wish them "Merry Christmas" and let them know he was thinking about them.

"It was always a special part of our Christmas morning," Sarah Nichols said, "leaving Dad on the phone in the other room as the rest of us got breakfast ready."

Alice Pruitt experienced a racing heart. Pruitt had been treated for depression for years, and she and others thought those episodes of heart palpitations that she described as "scary" were symptoms of some sort of panic attack.

During a regular checkup at the clinic, she said, "I've got another one coming on right now." Nichols put a stethoscope to her chest and determined it was a form of supraventricular tachycardia – an unusually fast heart rhythm triggered by a malfunction in the heart's electrical system.

"This isn't anxiety," Nichols told her. "It's an actual medical condition."

He treated the condition with medication, and she was fine. That was only one reason Pruitt was won over by Nichols. She had an innate fear of physicians, something she had overcome as a patient of others in the practice, first Dr. Robert Newman and then physician assistant Michelle Hass, but after they departed, Pruitt said she feared finding anyone she liked as much as them, and she was left to start over, apprehensively, with Nichols, but her anxiety didn't last long.

"Dr. Nichols was just so compassionate," Pruitt said. "He was just like family, so concerned whenever I'd go in. He knew how afraid I was of a doctor, so they always set me up with a 1 o'clock appointment, right after lunch, so they could call me right away. He'd always come in and kiss me on the jaw. When you have depression, that means a lot, especially when you're afraid of a doctor to start with."

Nichols listened like a friend, Pruitt said, when she would talk about her faith or her 18-year-old grandson who was killed a traffic crash.

"I can't talk about him without getting choked up, and Dr. Nichols would pat me on the leg and hug me and talk to me. I'd get to crying, and tears would come into his eyes."

She talked of hearing his helicopter flying in on Thursday mornings and standing on her sidewalk and waving to him as he came over her house. If Nichols were riding in a golf cart to the clinic and saw Pruitt, he would stop and chat and give her a hug. She framed a photograph of the two of them embracing and keeps it in her home.

"I could never tell what he's meant in my life," she said. "Never. He was always there. When he'd leave to go home, he'd say, 'If you need me, you've got my number. Call me.'"

Added Pruitt, "He will live forever in my heart."

At the 2008 groundbreaking for the new health center, shovels in hand, (from left) Jimmie Carter, Dr. David Nichols, Inez Pruitt, E. Carlton "Buddy" Wilton, Jr., B.H.B. Hubbard III and Lonnie Moore. *Ken Touchton*

TEN

A Leaky Roof, Kind Hearts
'Let's get a new clinic!'

*J*immie Carter is the definition of gregarious. Outgoing and friendly, James N. Carter Jr. – no relation to the former U.S. president of almost the same name – cuts a generous figure on the Northern Neck, in stature and personality. He seems always to be on the move, on the lookout for someone to meet, people to introduce. A real estate developer by occupation, and perhaps, by birth, as his parents operated a successful real estate firm in White Stone after moving their large family from Richmond, Carter is by nature and experience a consummate networker and a conciliator. Being the fourth-oldest of nine children with seven sisters and a brother provided unparalleled preparation.

Carter was 6 when his parents, Jim and Pat, decided to move full-time to the Northern Neck where they had a summer home. More than five decades later, Carter remains grateful for that relocation.

"There's something so lovely about living in a small community like this," said Carter, driving through White Stone on a summer afternoon. "I can't thank them enough for moving down here.

"There's something so nurturing about it. It just fits my personality. I love knowing everybody. I like the transparency of a small community, where if you're a good person, people know it. If you're [not], people know it. I like the accountability. Every day I wake up thinking I'm just the luckiest guy in the world to live here."

Carter's good fortune extended to his health, which has always been good, meaning he has been spared the need to spend a lot of time in doctors' offices, and he never got to know his longtime family physician all that well. He knew David Nichols more as an investor in real estate than as a doctor. Nichols had made a significant sum buying and selling real estate over the years. He was a shrewd businessman who was as thorough with his investments as he was with his patients. Friends said Nichols made his living in medicine, but he made his money in real estate.

It was a potential real estate deal that brought Carter and Nichols together in 2005. Nichols was considering buying a piece of waterfront property in a development on the Rappahannock River managed by Carter. Nichols wanted to visit the site, so the two of them flew there in his helicopter. They looked around for a while and talked.

"Let's go to lunch," Nichols said.

They thought about flying to Williamsburg to eat, considered another place or two, and then Carter, knowing of Nichols' work on Tangier Island, said, "Let's go to Tangier!"

Years later, Nichols would say he had "no ulterior motive, no agenda" in flying Carter to Tangier. "Just a fun thing to do," he said. There's no reason to believe otherwise. Yet, there also is no way to dispute Carter's retrospective view: "Funny how little things tip the balance."

Before that day in 2005, Carter had visited Tangier maybe a half-dozen times over the years, but he'd never gone there with Nichols. He knew the island, but as he quickly discovered, he didn't know it, or as he put it, "I had an appreciation for it, but didn't have any real connection to it."

So Nichols flew Carter across the bay. They landed at the airfield and walked through town to Hilda Crockett's Chesapeake House where they pulled up chairs for the usual massive lunch spread, served family-style: crab cakes, clam fritters, Virginia ham, potato salad, pickled beets, corn pudding, coleslaw, homemade rolls and more. They talked about Nichols' work on the island, and Nichols shared how attached he felt to the place. Carter listened, but he could see it even more clearly in the way people greeted Nichols with a combination of kinship and near reverence.

Lunch over, Carter asked Nichols to show him where he worked, so they walked to the clinic. Nichols opened the door to the weather-beaten building, and Carter was appalled. The interior was dark and cramped, and those were among its more tolerable features. The ceiling tiles were stained from rainwater leaking through the roof, and the aroma of mildew was everywhere; the toilet was about to fall through the floor; and Nichols mentioned the heat didn't work well, so when the weather turned cold he could not only hear patients' breath when he asked them to inhale deeply and exhale, he could *see* it.

"I don't think he understood how bad it was because he'd gotten used to it," said Carter, who told Nichols, "This is terrible! How can you operate efficiently out of here?"

And then, at once aghast and inspired, Carter blurted, "Let's get a new clinic!"

It's not that Nichols hadn't had the same thought many times before, but he knew such an undertaking would require a huge sum of money – hundreds of thousands of dollars, at least – that was far beyond the means of the people of Tangier, and he didn't have it in him to ask anyone off the island for help. Carter had no such qualms, and he had arrived at a point in his life where he was seeking a challenge, maybe even one beyond his typical reach.

It happened quickly; five minutes after walking into the rundown clinic, Nichols and Carter struck a deal that they would build a new one, though they left the island that day not knowing exactly how.

Carter is not easily daunted. He once bicycled across America. He traveled through the Arctic Circle on a dog sled, sleeping in tents when it was 20 degrees below zero. He even had a Tangier adventure under his belt: as a young man, he and a buddy paddled canoes across the bay to the island – in December. They showed up on the island pretty much with icicles hanging off them (they hitched a boat ride back to the mainland), but this promise he made about the clinic was something beyond even his most ambitious undertakings.

"I came home and said, 'Oh my God, what have I gotten myself into?'" Carter said. "My biggest fear was I wasn't going to live up to my responsibility of saying I was going to do this thing. I'd never done anything like this. I just didn't want to fail."

Carter was stirred to get involved and to succeed, in part, because of personal experience. His father had died in 2005 after what Carter described as a "lousy end-of-life experience." As a result, Carter felt compelled to do *something* to improve medical care. He didn't know what or for whom or just how – until that day on Tangier. He didn't go looking for Tangier, but he was receptive when it found him.

"I was itching to do something," Carter said. "I was in my mid-50s, and I was looking for personal purpose, and I had just gotten it straight in my mind that I wanted to do health care. I can't figure out how to cure AIDS, but I felt like I could get my arms around Tangier."

He added, "What I didn't know at the beginning was what that day was going to mean to me. It was one of the greatest events of my life. Getting to know the islanders and getting to see David's unique passion."

Nichols and Carter discussed what a new clinic should include. They put together a wish list and crunched the numbers: in a perfect world, they would need to raise $1.2 million for what they wanted to build. Then they got to work.

The day after he promised Nichols they would build a new health center, Carter hired an assistant, Nancy Thorsen, to get started on the project. They started writing letters and laying the groundwork for a fundraising campaign. They established the nonprofit Tangier Island Health Foundation, and board members were appointed from off the island and on.

"We just figured if we stayed in motion, the motion would breed success," Carter said. "We just kept hitting it, and things just started. It wasn't as if we knew what we were doing. But it was such a compelling story, and he was a very compelling person."

A critical turning point in the project came very early. On one of her first days on the job, Thorsen came into the office and said while watching a network news broadcast the previous evening she had seen a segment featuring a physician who had been honored as "Country Doctor of the Year."

"I don't know what that means," she said, "but I just thought I'd point it out to you."

"I know what it means," Carter replied, the wheels already turning. "It means we're going to win 'Country Doctor of the Year' for our guy next year."

Years later, Carter would say Thorsen (who later married, became Nancy Stanley and eventually left the job) and her successor, Tina Hagen, were "amazing."

"I give both of these women great credit for their contributions," he said. "The thing never would have happened as smoothly as it did without what they brought to the table. This was a passion for them. It was more than a job. They were lovely in their approach to this."

Carter and Thorsen researched the award and dis-covered it was presented annually by Staff Care, a Texas-based medical staffing company that had been honoring dedicated primary care physicians in rural areas since the 1990s. Not long after, they nominated Nichols for the following year's award – actually, Inez Pruitt wrote the lead nomination – but they didn't tell Nichols because Carter and the others knew he never would have gone for the idea.

"He was so humble he would never give himself credit," said Clark, his assistant. He cared nothing for the spotlight and was totally uncomfortable in the realm of self-promotion. Though he was controlling in many ways, he preferred sharing credit for his success with colleagues, and he was unnerved by the notion of being a nominee for the award once it became clear he was a finalist, but he agreed to do it if it might help Tangier.

The process was thorough, including interviews and site visits by a selection committee, and at one point Nichols told Clark, "Kim, I'm never good at stuff like this." So she pumped him with encouragement and suggested talking points and even sat across the desk from him in his office for emotional support when he did an initial phone interview with the selection committee.

In the end, Nichols' work tending to the medical needs of the island was most persuasive – who could resist a story of people living on a dot of an island in the middle of the bay and the doctor who cared for them? – and he was chosen as the 2006 "Country Doctor of the

The Nichols family at the 2006 Country Doctor of the Year award ceremony: Ivana and Davy, Sarah, David and Dianne.
Nichols family

Year." The honor belonged to Nichols, but the benefit went to Tangier.

News coverage of Nichols receiving the award allowed his story to reach a wider audience, including government officials in Richmond and potential donors across Virginia and beyond. Perhaps the biggest coup came in January 2007 when he was selected as the ABC News Person of the Week and featured on the national evening news.

The award and ensuing news coverage stamped Nichols with added credibility and provided instant momentum to the fledgling effort to build a new health center. Carter and Nichols were off and running.

They went on a speaking circuit of churches and Rotary Clubs and any other group that would care to listen. Their standard presentation included a slideshow about Tangier with Nichols talking about his work and the island. That was the agreement: Nichols would tell the story, and Carter would ask for the money.

"I don't like to ask people for things," Nichols said. As a negotiator, his business contacts affirmed without hesitation and with admiration, he was cold-blooded, single-minded and relentless – though unceasingly polite – in his pursuit of the lowest price. To flat-out ask for something? He was completely ill at ease doing that. However, he didn't mind in the least presenting the Tangier story if it would help get what he wanted.

"Once he got the recognition and he saw how it was helping Tangier, he was loving it," Clark said. "Not the recognition, but the help for Tangier. He wanted you to love Tangier like he loved Tangier. I would often comment to people, 'You just have to experience Tangier through his eyes.'"

He liked nothing better than introducing audiences to this tiny island in the bay. He would talk about how deeply he cared for the island and how difficult it was to deliver appropriate medical care to the people of Tangier and how desperately they needed a new facility that wasn't falling in on them. It was pretty clear, wher-ever Carter and Nichols went to speak, how captivated audiences were with the doc's passion and dedication. And when anyone wanted a close-up view, Nichols was only too happy to fly them over and introduce them to the island, Inez, and most dramatically, the old clinic.

"When they showed you the clinic, it's the old deal: don't take your checkbook to the dinner," E. Carl-ton "Buddy" Wilton Jr. said with a laugh.

Wilton, a Richmond-born developer and philan-thropist, went to school on the Northern Neck and had a home there, on the bay at the entrance to the Little Wic-omico River. From the widow's walk of his home, he can see the lights of Tangier. Over the years, he would occa-sionally take his boat to Tangier, carry visitors over to see what a traditional island in the bay looks like. He loved the way the islanders talked, and he admired how they had clung to their traditions and heritage and way of life. But he really didn't start getting to know the islanders un-til he went over to Tangier with Nichols and Carter, who was a longtime friend who had been the best man at both of Wilton's weddings. Carter told Wilton he was raising money to build a new health center on Tangier, and in-vited him to fly over to the island with him and Nichols.

"You walked into the [old] clinic and said, 'Whoa!'" Wilton said. "If the ceiling didn't fall on you, you would step through a hole in the floor. Those were your two options."

But it wasn't just the state of the clinic that attracted Wilton to the project. It was Nichols. They walked the streets of Tangier, and Wilton was struck by how everyone knew Nichols and he knew them, but not just in a 'Hi-howya-doin?' way; he had saved their life or the life of someone they loved, and the doctor and the people of this island were bound forever. Wilton was sold. Organizations often ask for his help, but as charitable requests go, this one was easy.

"He could sell ice to an Eskimo," Wilton said. "He didn't make you do anything; you just *wanted* to do it for him. The stories he could tell. The lives he had touched. He gave you the opportunity to be involved, and that was it."

Nichols' genuine but low-key manner, his unyielding yet subtle approach proved to be the linchpin of the project. Carter described him as "very disarming" with "no flash whatsoever."

"But," Carter said, "he had a good way of just cutting through to people."

Nichols had three qualities in particular that Julien G. Patterson noted right off.

"He was gentle, he was kind and he was sincere," said Patterson. "He was genuine in all three areas, which I don't think is something you find much these days."

Patterson, chairman and founder of a security company, OMNIPLEX World Services Corp., is a part-time resident of the Northern Neck. He did not know Nichols until he went to lunch at the Car Wash Café, a popular eatery in a former gas station in Kilmarnock, and ran into Carter, whom he'd met after delivering a speech before an area group. Nichols was with Carter – they were in the early stages of the project – and he brought Nichols over to meet Patterson.

"He shook my hand," Patterson said, "but then he put his hand on my shoulder. Just a gentle kind of thing. He and Jimmie started to tell me about the clinic, and then David said, 'Let's go! I'll take you over right now!'"

Patterson couldn't go that afternoon, but he was struck by Nichols' enthusiasm, and he promised to take him up on the offer another time, which arrived on a Saturday when Patterson and his wife, Terri, ran into Nichols, who offered to fly them to Tangier that very day. They accepted, drove to Nichols' home and climbed aboard his helicopter.

"He showed us a great time," said Patterson, who has worked around the world and designed specialized security training programs for the Central Intelligence Agency. "As we were going over, he told us the story about when he first went over and what his promise was and how important it was to him to keep his promise. It was just incredible. You thought, 'What's driving this?

Can he possibly have this much passion for these men
and women?' When we landed it became perfectly obvious."

The Pattersons had never been to Tangier, so Nichols gave them a tour. He took them to lunch at Hilda
Crockett's, he walked them over to the clinic, of course,
and he introduced them to Inez Pruitt and her family
and to other islanders along the way. They saw the deep,
personal connections Nichols had with the Tangiermen.
They witnessed the hugs and the handshakes. They met
watermen and heard their stories about learning their
trade from their fathers and grandfathers.

"His agenda was simple," Patterson said of Nichols. "All he asked you to do was come and see. Come
and see. It was almost a Biblical sort of thing, you know?
'Come and see Tangier. Meet the people.' That was the
magic. Because once you got involved and you saw his
passion and you saw the great need ... you understood
what it meant for them to have health care. There are no
amusement parks, no McDonalds. There's just a history
and a culture and a simplicity of life. A wonderful simplicity of life that is golden.

Absolutely golden. You wanted to do everything
you could to make the dream possible. It just resonated
with me, and I think it resonated with a lot of people."

At the groundbreaking in October 2008, the Pattersons provided Nichols and Carter seed money – $50,000

from a family foundation – to ensure the future viability of the new health center. They were among hundreds of donors – from business leaders to Girl Scouts, many of whom knew nothing or almost nothing about Tangier but had come to know the *story* – to join the effort. Carter said he had never truly appreciated the power of small donations until he became involved in the clinic project.

"You get all these solicitations, and you're embarrassed if you don't send at least $100," he said. "But what I found out during this process is I don't care if it's $2. The power of having community support behind you and being able to show the number of donors you've got and the grassroots support really greases the skids for public and foundation support."

Carter called on longtime connections, such as Virginia Gov. Tim Kaine, a Democrat, who was so moved by the project he sought $200,000 from the General Assembly to help launch the project; Republican State Sen. John Chichester, chairman of the Senate Finance Committee, responded by kicking in almost half as much again, so that in 2008 the Tangier Island Health Foundation received a state appropriation of about $300,000 in the form of a challenge grant. The foundation had to match with fundraising for the state money to be released, which surprisingly proved not to be such a daunting task. Carter navigated his way around the world of private foundations, tapping into sources of funding that helped propel the project from concept to reality more quickly than anticipated.

The fundraising was proceeding steadily, nearing $800,000, when Nichols mentioned to Carter he had heard something about community block grants from the U.S. Department of Agriculture. Nichols didn't seriously consider them, but Carter did not want to leave any door unopened. He looked into the grants and applied. Meetings were held, paperwork submitted and bureaucracy navigated. It was a complicated, painstaking and not altogether smooth process – Nichols not being the most patient participant when it came to the sometimes plodding pace of such an exercise – but the grant came through: $700,000. *$700,000!* It was a remarkable development. Worried at one point whether they would reach their goal of $1.2 million, Carter and Nichols suddenly found themselves well beyond their wildest dreams. The USDA money capped off the fundraising to build the health center – straight off Nichols' construction wish list.

The timing of it all could hardly have worked out better. Had the agriculture department's grant arrived sooner in the process, Carter said other donors might have sensed a diminished urgency in the fundraising and given less or none at all. Now though, the foundation would have money left over after construction to grow the endowment that would make certain their efforts would endure and high-quality medical care on Tangier would continue long into the future.

But then the timing was favorable throughout the
venture. When Carter and Nichols started raising money,
the economy was good and there was money to be found
in both the private and public sectors. A couple of years
later, the economy tanked, and fundraising became a
nightmare for nonprofits, but Carter and Nichols had
the money they needed, and it was time to build. Once
again, the timing couldn't have been more advantageous.
Construction work was scarce, so builders were eager
for jobs and submitted bids that were below what Carter
and Nichols expected, as much as hundreds of thousands
of dollars less. It was stunning how well everything had
fallen into place. On top of everything else, two major
bequests eventually will bring the foundation another
$1.5 million.

Carter and Nichols had transformed a shared
dream of building a health center on an island into a
textbook example of a public-private partnership working
to solve a local problem. Big money came from federal
and state grants and private foundations, but it was the
generosity of private individuals, churches, civic groups
and community organizations that kick-started the project in terms of money and momentum. And it wasn't just
money people were giving. They donated time, goods
and services, they held bake sales, happy to be involved
in one way or another.

McGuire Woods Consulting, a Richmond firm, was
instrumental in navigating the process that ended with the

foundation securing the state grant; B.H.B. Hubbard III, an Irvington attorney, handled all of the legal work for the new clinic; Nancy Dykeman, a Gloucester certified public accountant, handled the accounting work.

"I don't think you'd find a foundation where there's been less costs," Carter said. "There was so much help given us; it was heartwarming."

When it came to the actual construction, David A. Jones played a key behind-the-scenes role. Jones, president of Connemara Corp., a White Stone construction firm, didn't want to build the center – he told Carter and Nichols up front that someone else could do it less expensively – but he agreed to serve as an unpaid liaison between the foundation and the contractor, which turned out to be Southern Builders Inc. of Salisbury, Md. Jones sat on the foundation board and helped Carter and Nichols determine what they wanted built, and then he made sure the health center was built the way they wanted it. He helped review the bids and assisted in negotiations. He kept an eye on the construction, double-checked bills, and managed change-orders and punch lists.

His involvement brought an expertise to the process that took pressure off Carter and Nichols, and in some ways, the builder. Nichols often would quiz the contractor about why he didn't have more people on the job or why something wasn't finished. Patience was not one of his stronger virtues, so Jones would intervene to assuage Nichols.

"I said, 'Doc, they gave us a contract and a schedule, and they're meeting their schedule,'" Jones said.

Jones had known Nichols since the 1970s when the physician first came to the Northern Neck. Jones knew him as a patient in his practice and as a builder. When he was a young man starting out in the business, Jones was on the crew that built a screen porch at Nichols' home. Nichols had been highly involved in that project, too. So Jones knew what he was getting into. Sort of.

"He was a nice guy, but he worried you to death about *everything,*" Jones said with a laugh, describing his first impression of Nichols from working on the porch project. Others, who knew Nichols from the later construction of a family home on the Rappahannock or the building of a medical office in White Stone that opened in 2000, would vouch for Jones' words.

"My whole life with him was always that way," Jones said. "It was always going to be his way – and if you weren't doing your health the way he thought you should, he let you know about that."

From a medical standpoint, Nichols had helped Jones through difficult times. In his late 30s, Jones was diagnosed with prostate cancer by another physician. For a second opinion, he visited Nichols, who ran his own tests and said he thought the diagnosis was incorrect. He sent Jones to a urologist in Richmond.

"I think everything's going to be OK," Nichols told him. The original diagnosis proved to be a false alarm.

Nichols also diagnosed Jones' mother with cancer. "He'd been on my mom for years to quit smoking," Jones said. "She never showed any signs of [cancer], but he kept telling her, 'It's going to get you one day.' She died at age 60. He was very matter of fact, but very compassionate. He was the same with my prostate problems. He was genuinely concerned."

Over the years, Jones had gotten to know the business side of Nichols, too, through his public roles: Jones has served as vice-mayor of White Stone and the town's zoning administrator, as well as chairman of the Lancaster County Planning Commission and a member of the White Stone Volunteer Fire Department. He had helped broker a deal between the town and Nichols for White Stone to purchase the physician's original medical building and use it as the town's government offices. Another time, they were investors in a business deal that went south. Nichols became so frustrated that he stopped attending meetings and turned over his voting rights to Jones.

"He just didn't have the temperament for it," Jones said, recounting how Nichols kept trying to come up with ways to resolve the situation without losing their money. "He called me one night, and I said, 'It's gone, Doc.' He finally gave up, but he did not want to fail at anything."

"Tenacious" is how Jones described Nichols, most especially when it came to the new health center on Tangier.

Jones became involved with the Tangier health center in the same way so many others did. One day he was chatting with Nichols or Carter – he can't remember which one – when it was casually mentioned they were working on a new clinic for the island and they might want to call him for advice, and the next he was sitting at one of the long tables at Hilda Crockett's, helping himself to platters of hush puppies and clam fritters, neck-deep in the project and wondering, "How the hell did this happen?"

Jones possesses a wicked sense of humor with an endless stream of one-liners and wisecracks, a perfect foil to Nichols' seemingly serious, obsessive approach to life (though in truth Nichols had a well-cultivated sense of humor and could be downright goofy at times). Jones bought into the project, agreeing to donate his time and energy, because he liked Nichols so much and because Carter "is such a nice guy you can't tell him no."

"I would like to be able to sit here and tell you I did it for the people on Tangier," Jones said. "I didn't. I did it for Dr. Nichols and Jimmie – and grew into wanting to do it for the people on Tangier."

Tangier is not the easiest place to build anything. There are no builders' supply stores on the island, no heavy equipment. For any significant construction project, everything and pretty much everyone has to be brought in. The original idea for the new clinic was to build a foundation and a basic framework and then ship in prefabricated, modular sections that would be set in place by crane. The turnaround would be quick, and they thought, easy.

But on closer inspection the modular sections were too wide and heavy for the narrow lanes and small bridges on the island. To make the necessary modifications and arrangements would have been prohibitively expensive, so the decision was made to build the clinic conventionally: from the ground up.

Construction began in late 2009, and though complicated by the sheer logistics, the construction went "exactly as we expected," Jones said.

Everything – from gravel to shingles to any necessary equipment – had to be brought over on barges and other boats. A track-loader picked up everything at the dock and then maneuvered to the building site despite extremely tight fits on roadways more accustomed to golf carts and scooters. Without concrete-mixing trucks, the concrete was brought in dry, in huge bags, then dumped in a portable mixer and poured from a forklift bucket.

"The logistics weren't as bad as you would think," Jones said. "We hired a company that had worked on the island before so they knew how to get on and off. They knew what they were doing."

The builders became familiar faces on the island; you can't work on such a big project in such a small place without becoming part of the community. The people of Tangier embraced the workers, bringing them cookies and doughnuts and treating them like family. As the building progressed and the health center took shape, the excitement on and off the island grew.

The health center, just around the corner from the old clinic and built on property purchased from Dewey and Jean Crockett, was designed by Irvington architect Bill Prillaman to fit in aesthetically with its island sur-roundings; it has the look of a well-appointed beach cottage with its wide, welcoming front porch and sunny colors. But it is something much more. It is perhaps five times larger than the old clinic with numerous examina-tion rooms, state-of-the-art equipment such as a digital X-ray machine and a wireless Internet connection, a spa-cious waiting room with comfortable chairs, and niceties such as artwork and an upstairs apartment for visiting physicians. The place was built with offices for Nichols and Pruitt, the name plates outside the respective doors offering not only their actual names but these: "Wilbur" and "Homer."

"I honestly believe there's not a more modern clinic for family medicine anywhere in this country," Nichols said as the building was about to open.

The place would be well-equipped so it could handle almost any medical situation that would arise, and it was built large, said Carter, to efficiently take advantage of weekly visits by mainland physicians. With numerous exam rooms, a considerable number of patients could be accommodated in a single day.

The health center was designed and built with its location in mind: a low-lying island where flooding as a proposition is not an "if" but a "when." To that end, the structure stands on pillars several feet above the ground and has the highest clearance of any building on the island; so high, in fact, if flood waters ever reached the front door of the clinic, chances are the rest of the island would be a lost cause.

However, Nichols, ever obsessive about details, believed the health center should be built 8 inches higher. Jones told him that would be totally unnecessary; it already was more than high enough.

"I said, 'Doc, you don't need it,'" Jones said.

Nichols was adamant, but Jones was more so. Jones prevailed, but Nichols insisted his objection be placed in the minutes of the foundation meeting.

Jones shook his head and laughed at the memory. Nichols was very even-tempered as a physician, Jones said, "But he could really get his burr up if things didn't go his way. He was never mean about it, but he was always direct."

That was Nichols' way. It was nothing personal.

"He expected the best out of people and didn't take less than that," Carter said. "He made people hold to the highest level of integrity and service. David was very demanding of people. When you worked for David, there was no cutting corners. There was accountability. It was fascinating to see how he worked."

Carter and Nichols had been acquaintances when the process of building the health center started; over those five years, they became the closest of friends. But then Carter had come through big-time for Nichols. He had put together a formidable organization to achieve what just a few years earlier could only have been described as an admirable fantasy. He had shepherded personal passion, public goodwill and astute business and political networking into a remarkable project that was on the verge of reaching completion: an impossible dream come true.

"Jimmie, in my mind, is a hero for what he did for the folks on Tangier and for David," said Bill Westbrook, an advertising executive, brand consultant, entrepreneur and author who lived on the Northern Neck at the time the health center was in the works but now lives primarily in Minnesota."Jimmie was the driver. He totally understood David and what David was doing, and Jimmie made it his mission to build that clinic. He discovered things about himself in the process that he never knew he could do.

"Jimmie doesn't truly ask anybody for anything. He lets you know what he's working on, and because he's Jimmie you sort of want to help him. That's what it was with me. As much as anything, I have such a love for Jimmie that I wanted to help him do anything he felt was worthwhile. And once I got involved with David and Inez, I could see it as clearly as the hand in front of my face how important it was."

Westbrook half-jokingly suggested he became involved initially because he and Carter were partners in White Fences Vineyard and Winery on the Northern Neck. "I got him into the vineyard," he said with a laugh, "and he got me into the clinic. Turnabout is fair play."

But there was more to it than that. Westbrook already had an appreciation for the watermen of the bay region and their plight, having established a foundation with the purpose of preserving the watermen's way of life. He felt a kinship to them through his father, who "worked with his hands," he said. "He took things apart and fixed them, and that's kind of like what watermen do. They work with their hands."

Westbrook knew Nichols as "the copter doctor" and as an occasional customer at the Trick Dog Café in Irvington, a restaurant Westbrook owned for a time. He was familiar with Nichols' work on Tangier, but like others who became involved in the project, did not know of the abysmal conditions of the island's clinic until he flew over with Nichols and Carter. The incidence of heart disease and other health issues on the island and the frequency of medical evacuation to the mainland sealed the deal for Westbrook's involvement.

"How do you say no to that?" he asked.

Westbrook not only helped the project financially (and "soulfully," as Carter put it) but he pulled artwork from his house to decorate the health center. He remains on the foundation's board.

"There's not a false note in the entire effort, not one false note," Westbrook said. "Not even the most cynical people could find anything to quibble about in raising money to help promote the health and well-being of their neighbors sitting on a speck in the middle of the bay. This was always about the people of Tangier. It was never about David Nichols."

But as construction of the health center neared completion in July 2010 and a happy ending came into view, the story took a bleak turn, and it became very much about David Nichols.

In April 2010, Nichols and Pruitt posed for a photo in front of the health center that was well under construction.
Bill Lohmann

Nichols waves to the crowd from the porch of the new health center named for him at the dedication of the facility August 29, 2010.
Bob Brown/Richmond Times-Dispatch

ELEVEN

THE NEWS IS BAD
'I will never leave you in spirit'

Nichols recalled a weary patient with advanced cancer showing up in the Tangier clinic saying he was "tired of being sick."

"I want to die peacefully," the man told Nichols.

He had been undergoing treatment off the island, away from home and away from family, and it just wasn't worth it, he said. Nichols spent most of a morning listening to the man, talking over his options, supporting his decision. When they were done, the patient cried on Nichols' shoulder.

Nichols hated to see patients with incurable cancers chase the false hope of difficult, experimental treatments, sometimes traveling all over the country at great expense. He counseled patients to take control of their treatment – weigh the prospects and the side effects – and he disliked specialists who exploited patients and their families by leading them down a path of unjustified optimism.

"There are some patients you just want to shake and say, 'Why are you doing this?'" he said. "I've seen so many people go down that road just constantly being made to feel hopeful when hope really was not there, when what they really ought to be concentrating on is the here and now and the reality of the situation. For God's sake, don't ruin the last few months of your life taking medicines that are just going to make you feel sick. Why not just stay at home and enjoy your life while you have it?"

Among the birthdays, anniversaries and other important dates running around in Kim Clark's head, there is this one: April 9, 2004. It was a Friday. She remembers it with perfect clarity because that was the day Nichols went for his annual eye exam, which typically wouldn't have been a big deal until what transpired the following Monday. Nichols arrived in the office and nonchalantly mentioned the examining physician thought he had ocular melanoma – a form of cancer of the eye – and then went about his morning routine as if nothing was amiss.

"You could have knocked me over with a feather," Clark said. "I had to corner him and ask, 'What is melanoma of the eye?' I didn't know what that was."

Most melanomas develop on the skin, but they can form elsewhere. Ocular melanoma is the most common primary cancer of the eye in adults, according to the Ocular Melanoma Foundation, but it's not all that common, diagnosed in about 2,500 adults every year in the United States. Older, lightly pigmented individuals seem to be most susceptible to ocular melanoma, which is an aggressive cancer that spreads to other parts of the body in about half of all cases and is often fatal. Exposure to ultraviolet rays increases the risk of developing melanoma of the skin, however there is no conclusive evidence linking exposure to ultraviolet rays to ocular melanoma, and the exact cause is unknown.

Still, Nichols couldn't help but wonder in later years if the three summers he worked as a lifeguard at Lake Ontario in the 1960s were the source of the cancer. He did not have the science to back up that suspicion, but his complexion was fair, and he recalled that he did not wear dark glasses or use sunscreen. He could not help but think back to those days as he tried to understand how he could have become afflicted with the disease.

Nichols saw a specialist in Richmond that afternoon, and the following week he was in Pennsylvania undergoing radiation treatment. Upon his return to White Stone, Nichols rarely discussed what had gone on – he allowed most friends and colleagues to believe he had a generic eye problem and simply had undergone a routine procedure to take care of it – and seldom let on to the seriousness of the situation.

"He didn't want sympathy," Clark said. "But he'd tell me all the time, 'Kim, I've done research. It's deadly. It's going to get me.'"

As with his patients, Nichols proved to be an astute diagnostician, even when the case involved his own health. He lived with that grim prospect for six years, almost never talking about it, an ominous weight he largely shouldered privately. Indeed, Nichols said years later he was shaken by the diagnosis and never recovered from his belief he was living with a terminal disease.

In late June 2010, Nichols attended the wedding of Clark's daughter Becky, and he was particularly and uncharacteristically ebullient, even dancing on the chairs – "I have the picture to prove it," Clark said – before the evening was over. This was a side of Nichols few of his friends ever saw. He was so conscious of his reputation that he would never "let his hair down" in public, said Clark, whose mother wondered if the doctor had enjoyed a cocktail or two. Clark laughed. He had not. Nichols did not drink alcohol. Others who attended the wedding commented to Clark they had never seen Nichols so happy, never seen him so full of life.

A week or so after the wedding, Nichols arrived at the office feeling poorly and complaining about shoulder pain, even turning down a chance to fly to Tangier with

Davy, a pilot himself, who was ferrying supplies to the clinic. That wasn't normal, thought Clark, who knew him well enough to know he rarely declined an opportunity to go flying with his son. Even more telling was this: Nichols seldom complained about ailments, preferring to bottle up whatever he was thinking. She sensed something was wrong, so she pinned him down and presented him with three choices, all of which involved having another staff member examine him. He relented, and the ensuing blood work didn't show anything, which was good news but maybe shouldn't have been. He had experienced abdominal pain earlier in the spring and now this. Nichols suggested the problems were viruses, but perhaps deep down, considering the foreboding he had been harboring for years, he recognized the pain for what it was: an ominous sign.

On July 15, members of his staff hosted a surprise lunch for him on Tangier at the not-quite-finished new medical center. Everyone laughed a lot, stories were told, a picture was made of Nichols and the others on the front porch. "It was just the greatest day," Clark said. "He was like a kid in a candy shop. Little did we all know that this would be his last day practicing in Tangier."

The next day was his scheduled ultrasound, a routine exam which in previous years had merely confirmed his cancer had not returned. This time, though, the scan showed the cancer had metastasized in his liver. At age 62, Nichols was dying.

Weeks later, on a visit to Tangier in early August, Nichols proudly showed off the nearly completed medical center to visitors, pointing out the countless amenities and talking about all it would mean to the people of the island. He wasn't asked about his condition, and he didn't volunteer any information. He didn't say anything about his situation until he walked over to the old clinic and started reminiscing about the old days, growing reflective as he sat in the ghostly quiet of the once-bustling waiting room.

"I have probably about four months," Nichols said very matter-of-factly. "That's the statistical analysis."

He looked around the decrepit old clinic and despite its appearance said he was "very nostalgic" about the old place.

"How can I not be? Lots of memories. Happiness and sadness. Really wonderful people. I've lived a good life, you know. I feel good about it. I feel blessed to have been a part of Tangier."

He suddenly changed the course of the conversation, looked up and nodded across the street toward Swain Memorial United Methodist, the church with the familiar steeple. He had one last wish, he said.

"I want to be buried over at that church, at the graveyard," Nichols said. "Just put my ashes there."

The declaration caught some by surprise. Though dearly loved on the island, Nichols had never lived there. The islanders knew he cared deeply for them, but they might not have realized just how deeply. His desire to make Tangier his final resting place showed unquestionably the depth of his feelings for the place and the people, and how determined he was to remain a part of the island forever – and to be available to keep an eye on things -- since the cemetery was between the church and the new health center.

What Nichols didn't publicly let on was what a crushing, heartbreaking disappointment this was for him: not being able to practice medicine in this relative palace of a medical center that he was so instrumental in getting built. If Yankee Stadium was "The House That Ruth Built," this would be "The House That Nichols Built." Yet, he wouldn't lift the first stethoscope, wouldn't set the first broken bone. He had so looked forward to its opening. Not only would it be a supreme place to practice medicine, but he also anticipated having more time and energy to devote to the people of Tangier. In August 2008, he had sold his lucrative White Stone Family Practice to Riverside Medical Group, a division of Riverside Health System based in Newport News. His plan was to retire from practicing in White Stone, but to continue serving Tangier indefinitely. It would be, he thought, an ideal arrangement: more time for family and for flying and for his friends on Tangier.

How cruel was this twist? He had made the difficult decision to step back from the practice he had created and nurtured and enjoy life more – and now this. The cancer had forced him to give up flying and to retire from practicing medicine altogether. The new clinic was not yet open, but in a sense, he was already gone.

"Sure, I'll miss not being a part of all that and being able to do all those things I planned to do," he said, maintaining his professionalism to the end and underplaying his disappointment. "But it's the journey that's counted for me, and gosh, this was so rewarding."

Nichols said he felt almost a familial responsibility to his Tangier patients, a true protective instinct to take care of his friends there as if they were his blood relatives. So there was comfort in seeing the new medical center nearing completion, knowing Inez would be there every day to care for the islanders in his absence and realizing Riverside had committed to providing physicians on a weekly basis to Tangier as part of the deal to purchase White Stone Family Practice. ("Oh, trust me, that was a deal-breaker," said Clark, who worked closely with Nichols during the two-year process of negotiating with prospective buyers. "If they didn't want Tangier, they didn't want us.")

Soon after he received the grim diagnosis in July but before it was widely known, Nichols had summoned Carter to his home. He offered no hint as to the reason, but Carter recalled thinking it must be "a game-changer" because Nichols said he needed first to talk to his children. Carter was not aware of the earlier diagnosis of ocular melanoma, so he was caught completely off-guard when Nichols told him he probably had only a few months to live.

Barely after dawn the next morning, Jones picked up the phone at his construction office and heard Carter telling him the stunning news that Nichols was dying. Jones told Carter it was too early in the day for bad jokes. Carter assured him this wasn't one.

"We've *got* to get that building finished," Carter told him.

The race now was to finish the new health center and hold the public celebration while Nichols was still able to attend and enjoy it. Punch lists were drawn up, arrangements were made. The grand opening had been planned for later in the fall, when the weather likely would be cooler and the building would undoubtedly be completed. But there was no telling how Nichols' health would be by then, so the new date for the event was set for Aug. 29, a Sunday. Like undertaking a major building project, scheduling a big event on Tangier is no easy task. The sheer logistics of bringing in large numbers of main-landers present all sorts of challenges. Boats were added to the daily ferry schedule, and pilots of small planes were enlisted to fly special guests to Tangier three- and four-at-a-time on the big day.

The team effort included some of the project's biggest donors, who worked the phones or rolled up their sleeves to make the day happen. Julien Patterson, who had contacts at the highest level of Virginia state government, helped persuade Gov. Bob McDonnell, despite a busy schedule, to give up part of his Sunday to attend with members of his family. Bill Westbrook loaded personal paintings and photographs on a ferry and delivered them to Tangier to decorate the clinic. Buddy Wilton, who as a developer didn't generally wield hammers and screwdrivers, arrived in Tangier a week before the opening of the clinic to help with the finishing touches: hanging paper-towel dispensers, assembling cabinets and stress-test machines, and running errands to the mainland.

"It gave me an opportunity to really meet the people who work there," said Wilton, who had joined the board of the Tangier Island Health Foundation. "I really got the feel of what it was about."

He added: "I knew I was going to get involved, but I didn't think I'd get as *attached* to Tangier as I did."

The clinic's grand opening turned out to be something much more than a ribbon-cutting for a new building. In many ways, it became a celebration of David Nichols, an opportunity for the islanders to say "thank you" and a chance for those not terribly familiar with Tangier to see first-hand the uncommon love between the

Nichols holds the "Country Doctor of the Decade" award he was presented at the dedication of the new health center.
Bob Brown/Richmond Times-Dispatch

physician and the island. It was a day of joy and sadness, pride and gloom, hugs, laughter and tears. In terms of attendance and emotion, it was, without doubt, one of the biggest days in the history of the small island.

That Sunday was typical for late August in the Chesapeake Bay: hot and humid. For one day, Tangier's population might have doubled, and its small airfield looked like a bustling airport as dozens of small planes and helicopters descended on it.

"It's a pretty big day for Tangier," said island resident Bruce Gordy, as he hustled to close the Tangier History Museum early so he could find a good vantage point for the ceremony. "It's great, but it's sad, too."

Hundreds – watermen side-by-side with deep-pocketed donors and political dignitaries – gathered outside the new health center in the sweltering heat. Some sat in folding chairs and golf carts; most stood, tightly bunched in the slender street that runs in front of the building, which bore a new sign that had been kept a secret from Nichols until this moment. It read: *David B. Nichols Health Center.*

The center's front porch was filled with local and state officials, including McDonnell and Congressman Robert J. Wittman. McDonnell said he made the trip simply "to shower more love" on Nichols.

In welcoming everyone, Tangier Mayor "Ooker" Eskridge stood at the top of the steps of the new clinic and said, "The Bible tells about God using certain people for certain jobs at certain times. Dr. Nichols, we appreciate all you've done and all you're doing, and we love you."

Nichols basked in the moment, seated on the porch beside his longtime friend and patient, Dewey Crockett, who delivered the opening prayer.

"He kept patting my hand, and I said, 'Doc, we're going to make it, we're going to make it,'" Crockett said. "He's a precious soul, I tell you."

School children sang "This Land Is Your Land." Representatives of Staff Care, the organization that chose Nichols as "Country Doctor of the Year" in 2006, came from Texas to present Nichols with its first "Country Doctor of the Decade" award. Elected officials bestowed resolutions and commendations upon him. The crowd listened politely to all of the accolades, all the while guzzling water and waving hand-held fans like you find in country churches. Despite best efforts, several people wilted in the relentless heat from dehydration and became the first patients treated in the new health center. All recovered.

Inez Pruitt talks about Nichols at the dedication of the new health center. Nichols listens along with (from left) Dewey Crockett, Gov. Bob McDonnell, Rep. Rob Wittman and Virginia Department of Health Commissioner Karen Remley.
Bob Brown/Richmond Times-Dispatch

Inez Pruitt paid tribute to her mentor, saying he inspired her to follow her calling. She praised his commitment and compassion, and said she was "the most blessed woman in the world."

"I wouldn't change a thing," she said, "except for time – and more of it."

Nichols clearly was overwhelmed by the turnout, and unavoidably, the certainty of his mortality. When it came his turn to talk, Nichols, his eyes red and his voice catching, told the gathering, "While I will leave you in body, I will never leave you in spirit."

Nichols (top left) listens to the Tangier Combined School children's choir, standing on the front steps of the new health center, as they sing "This Land is Your Land" during the dedication of the new facility.
Bob Brown/Richmond Times-Dispatch

After the ceremony, the crowd moved to the island's schoolhouse for a reception that was more of a community picnic – tables laden with soft-shell crabs, clam fritters and ham, as well as homemade salads and cakes. The cups of iced tea went fast. One of the kitchen volunteers, Hedy Bowden, grew up on the island and was trying to remember a bigger community event but couldn't. "This is the biggest I've seen," she said.

After the exhilaration of the grand-opening ceremony, a true measure in plain view of what Nichols had meant to the island, the ailing physician retreated into the sobering reality of the rest of his life and into an unfamiliar, uncomfortable role: patient. Being in control was a hallmark of his life, and his health now rendered him dependent on others. However, he did have control over at least one aspect of his circumstances. In counseling terminally ill patients over the years, he routinely laid out treatment options but also cautioned against trying to wring a few more weeks or months of life at the expense of the quality of those days. Now, he confronted those same decisions, and early on he chose to heed his words.

"I want to be comfortable with what life I have," he said soon after the July diagnosis. "I've done a lot of thinking about it. I've seen too many times patients were given chemotherapy or radiation only to ruin what quality they had. I just don't want that for me. I don't want to have misery for my last few months. I mean, I will eventually, but not for the good part at least. God willing. That's the operative word."

He did agree to immunotherapy treatment – he wasn't sold on it, he said, but family and friends thought it was worth a try – but after only two treatments he developed respiratory problems and wound up in a hospital emergency room. He quit the treatment, hoping his breathing might improve, but it didn't. As a physician, he was not altogether surprised, and he took the result in stride. He was accepting and philosophical, much like when he first learned the cancer had spread and his days likely were numbered. "I figured, well, time's up," he said, "and I started thinking of the good things in my life."

He spent the months following the grand opening of the new health center with his family, traveling to Tangier when he could and putting his affairs in order. Carter marveled at the almost clinical detachment Nichols exhibited in dealing with his own impending death. Though he was unable to tend to patients, Nichols remained involved in the operation of the clinic, to the extent he could, and in making certain the foundation would ensure future medical care for the island. It proved a happy distraction. Davy, who had left his job only a few weeks before the most recent diagnosis to attend graduate school, now had time to spend with his father, and he helped him mark things off his "bucket list," such as spending an afternoon in an F/A-18C Hornet flight simulator at Naval Air Station Oceana in Virginia Beach, arranged by family friend Lt. Peter Scheu, a Navy pilot and weapons school instructor whose first flight in a small plane was with Nichols to Tangier. "After that," Scheu said, "I was hooked. All I wanted to do was fly fighters for the Navy."

For someone who could pilot airplanes and helicopters and could understand all of the instruments associated with such flying machines, Nichols didn't have the easiest time with things like computers and cell phones. Yet he came to love keeping in touch with family, friends and colleagues by way of text-messages. He loved receiving texts and photos – once he figured out how to send and receive them on his phone, which came with a double-battery because he knew he would forget to charge it regularly. "He made me have the same kind of phone," Clark said with a laugh, "so I could teach him how to use it."

Nichols mostly made time for his family, visiting the family's new beach home in Corolla on the Outer Banks of North Carolina. In another mean twist, the house had been completed only months before his diagnosis. As with the health center, his primary home on the Rappahannock and the building that housed White Stone Family Practice, Nichols had kept a vigilant watch on construction of the beach house: researching building materials, noticing the smallest details, making sure the house was built just the way he wanted and that he got his money's worth. Now he wouldn't be around to enjoy it for long.

Though as her husband's time grew short, Dianne Nichols said she preferred to view it as "a gift of time." There had been so many times she had worried for his safety – such as when he traveled in questionable weather to reach Tangier – and he had survived. She felt fortunate, and now, at least, they had time to enjoy together. And to say goodbye.

As hard as he had worked over the years, Nichols
had decided as he grew older that he didn't want to "die
with his boots on," as he used to tell Clark, which was
one reason he had sold his practice to Riverside. But he
didn't want to take off the boots just yet. After the sale,
he had practiced every Thursday on Tangier, and until
his health began to fail, he regularly showed up at White
Stone Family Practice. So much for retirement. And even
when his health grew more fragile and he had difficulty
getting around, he still found a way to go into the office.

Under hospice care at home, Nichols, who was on
pain medication and not allowed to get behind the wheel
of a car, cajoled his home-care nurses to drive him to his
office, where Clark would turn around to find him standing in the doorway, holding his briefcase. He explained
that he'd told the nurse that Clark could take him home
when he was ready. Clark could only laugh.

"Probably no other hospice nurses on the planet
had to drop off their patients at their office," she said.

Even locked in a battle that looked increasingly
unwinnable, Nichols tried to maintain a stoic front, de-
flecting attention away from himself, trying to make others feel better. Bob Newman, his friend and former colleague, fretted over making what was sure to be a painful
long-distance phone call to Nichols after learning about
his diagnosis. 'What do you say?" Newman thought.

"After mustering the courage to make the call, intending to comfort him, I came away from the conversation feeling better," Newman said. "That's the type of person he was. He even joked that he wouldn't now have to worry about dementia and the frailties of old age."

Yet for all of his outward optimism and can-do attitude about so many things, Nichols didn't try to fool himself. On occasion, when he and Clark were talking about matters involving the office, he would say things like, "In January, when I'm gone …" before, at her insistence, he would rephrase whatever he was saying in a less ominous context. He couldn't help himself; he was a realist. During his illness, he received scores of cards and long, lovely letters from patients that deeply moved him. He told Clark it seemed like he was "getting my sympathy cards before I die."

There were Christmas cards and heartfelt letters from his friends on Tangier, thanking him for the care he provided their parents, their children and themselves, likening him to a father figure or a brother. They sent him prayers and good wishes, and occasionally, money. Islander Betty McMann, who had been a patient and an employee and was confronting her own health issues at the time, tucked a $5 bill inside a get-well card. "Buy some jelly beans," she wrote. "They're colorful and sweet and easy to eat. Maybe you'll gain a lb. or two."

The mail brought a handwritten note from Virginia's governor. "As you fight the battle," Gov. McDonnell wrote, "know Virginia is grateful for your service and a better place because of your life."

In the years since the Country Doctor of the Year Award, Nichols' story had been featured in the mass media: The Washington Post, Parade, National Public Radio. As word got out about his illness in the Richmond Times-Dispatch and other news outlets around Virginia and then nationwide, he heard from people, many of whom he didn't know, from all over the country: Nevada, New York, Missouri, Colorado.

NBC's Nightly News with Brian Williams spotlighted Nichols in its "Making a Difference" segment. Williams described the report as "bittersweet."

"It's about a man who saw a need, committed himself to filling it and helped save more than a few lives along the way," Williams said in setting up the piece that aired Oct. 20, 2010.

Soon after, a letter arrived on notebook paper from 14-year-old Megan Abernathy of Plymouth, N.H., who had learned about Nichols and his work on Tangier from a network news program.

"It truly moved me," she wrote. "I found it so admirable how dedicated you had become. I was so devastated when they said you had been diagnosed with cancer.

I'm not usually one to cry during the news, but your story really got to me. I wish more people could be like you … Your story has inspired me to look at the bigger picture and ask myself what I can do to help others around me.

"In school you are always asked who your hero is. People answer with things like Abe Lincoln or Lance Armstrong. I had never really known what to say. I didn't know who inspired me to try harder or reach out to others. But, now I know. You are my hero."

As a result of the news coverage, Nichols received numerous letters from well-wishers around the country. He was determined to reply to each, said his daughter, Sarah, who helped him organize his correspondence and include a commemorative Tangier Island coin with each letter.

During his illness, Nichols also received a letter from Winston-Salem, N.C., from Dr. W. Gregory Hundley, a cardiologist and professor of internal medicine and radiology at the Wake Forest University School of Medicine. Nichols and Hundley had not been in touch for more than two decades, and even then only briefly. Hundley was a student from the Medical College of Virginia in Richmond performing a family practice/internal medicine rotation at Rappahannock General Hospital in Kilmarnock during the summer of 1986 when he had the opportunity to fly to Tangier a few times with Nichols. Hundley had learned of Nichols' illness when his mother sent him a Richmond newspaper clipping about the physician and his diagnosis.

"I wanted you to know that I greatly appreciated the opportunity to have worked with you," Hundley wrote. "The dedication and level of commitment to your patients in that community made a mark on my life and contributed to much of the work that I perform today."

Hundley went on to write that he was at work developing efficient and cost-effective ways to use imaging sciences for the improvement in health care and that what he had witnessed that summer helped shape his approach to medical care. Later, in an interview, Hundley recounted his eye-opening visits to Tangier, starting with the bouncy landings on the then-deteriorating island airstrip.

"The plane would go and touch down and hop up in the air and touch down and hop up and finally come to a stop," Hundley recalled with a laugh. "He said, 'Oh, we'll be OK.'"

Hundley never forgot how that unflappability carried over into the clinic. He was struck, all those years later, by the patients lined up at the clinic when they arrived, and how full – and fulfilling – the days were on the island.

"Every case was dramatic," he said. "Some of them would be really sick. It was constant triage. He was just really calm and got everything dealt with appropriately."

Hundley also remembered the way Nichols and his nurses made the best of less-than-ideal circumstances. He still marveled at the island clinic's old X-ray machine, which had been dismantled and brought over in pieces, then set atop a stack of old encyclopedias, its height adjusted by adding or removing volumes as necessary. Hundley remembered the improvisation as "a wonderful thing."

Looking back, he came to admire Nichols' resourcefulness and his ability to astutely size up a situation and the way he instinctively knew when to send a patient off the island for specialized treatment and when not to. That summer emphasized the essence of medical care to Hundley – "What's our mission as physicians?" he asked. "To take care of people" – but also drove home the point, on a very basic level, of the importance of treating patients compassionately and working step-by-step to quickly and accurately determine a diagnosis.

Hundley acknowledged his eyes "were like saucers" when Nichols would send him into a room to make an initial examination of a patient, enrolling him in a condensed version of the Nichols School of Hard Knocks.

"Good grief," Hundley thought at those times, "what am I going to do with this?"

But Nichols would lay out the situation, give Hundley a crash course in the patient's medical background and what needed to be done, and then assure him he would be back in a few minutes to check on things.

"And everything turned out well," Hundley said. "The patients got great care. Just great care."

Dianne and David Nichols walk into the sunset following
the dedication of the new health center.
Ken Touchton

On one of his final trips to the island, Nichols visits with Virginia "Ginny" Marshall in November 2010 at Lorraine's, the year-round island restaurant operated by Marshall's daughter.
Bill Lohmann

TWELVE

SAYING GOODBYE
'Mud between his toes'

*T*he November morning broke crisp and clear, pulling back the curtain on a magnificent scene made even more dazzling from the privileged vantage point of 1,500 feet above it all.

The creeks and coves of Virginia's coast stitch together a quilted landscape of forests, farms and neighborhoods. Out on the bay, sunlight danced across the sparkling water as fishermen and flocks of birds congregated in search of the same treasure. An occasional boat on the move cut a glistening and mesmerizing path.

David Nichols had witnessed this spectacle hundreds of times, maybe thousands, yet he never tired of it. From the passenger seat in his single-engine plane, he gazed with a silent joy until his eyes locked onto a tiny tuft of land in the distance, all alone in the bay, and his spirit lifted even more.

"Glorious," he said in hushed exclamation. "Paradise."

As Tangier Island drew closer, Nichols could see the homes where so many of his patients and friends lived, the crab shanties and small shops where they worked, the freshly painted blue water tower that along with the steeple of historic Swain Memorial United Methodist Church loomed large over this low-lying wisp of precious earth. The island's airstrip, hugging Tangier's western shore, beckoned his plane.

But Nichols saw something much more and felt something much deeper. He had grown to like saying when on Tangier "you're a little closer to heaven." He had begun traveling to Tangier from his mainland home more than 30 years earlier as a once-a-week mission, though he was not the second coming of Albert Schweitzer, and never claimed to be; he was operating a medical practice, not a free clinic. But he never made money practicing medicine on Tangier. In fact, he lost significant sums every year, though he managed to find ways to write off some of the costs. Make no mistake, however; he was a medical angel to the people of Tangier.

Somewhere along the way, Tangier came to represent something far more profound to Nichols than a worthy excuse to set off in flight over the bay once a week. He developed a deep love for the place and the people that wasn't necessarily clear unless you witnessed Nichols in action on Tangier or talked to those islanders who were his patients and became part of his extended family. If you knew Nichols only on the mainland as a gifted doctor and shrewd businessman, you quite possibly missed the depth of his feeling for Tangier and the place's hold on him. He was the same physician wherever he went, the same man, but on Tangier he seemed more relaxed, more at ease. He very much felt at home among the people, plainspoken and unpretentious who maintain a genial but somewhat wary view of outsiders.

There's a saying on Tangier that someone from away who comes to know the island and truly love it – squishy marsh muck and all – gets "mud between their toes." In a metaphorical sense, Nichols found himself knee-deep in the mud over the years, though the only times he could recall actually taking off his shoes and socks on Tangier were when extraordinarily high tides washed over the island, requiring him to wade back to the airstrip and his plane or helicopter. He couldn't recall, but even when he removed his shoes he probably never unknotted his necktie, and it probably never even occurred to him to do so.

On days he was seeing patients, he always wore a necktie. His work uniform his entire career was a short-sleeve, button-down shirt with tie under his lab coat.

Nichols was not one to make fashion statements, but he was an inveterate collector of ties. He had a closetful of neckties, hundreds of ties, many of them gifts from patients, and he loved wearing ties with motifs related to medicine, children, dogs, and of course, flying. The island certainly wasn't a place where neckties were required or where many men ever wore them, but Nichols felt obliged to uphold his professional sense of decorum, and that included neckties, even on the steamiest of summer days.

Though the income from his mainland practice and his real estate investments provided a comfortable living, Nichols was not the country-club type. He admired the lack of materialism among the people of Tangier and was awed by their devotion to their faith, their families and their island home, despite whatever hardships came in the bargain, including limited access to medical care. As a result, they had needed Nichols, and it turned out that he needed them, too. Now at age 62, white-haired, easy-going and soft-spoken with a hint of his Canadian upbringing, Nichols had, in many ways, become one of them. His genuine dedication to the island and its people was unquestioned. In fact, islanders jokingly suggested his name should be changed to David Nichols *Parks*, the most prominent surname on the island of about 500 residents. It made him smile, and it made him proud.

Beyond the people, Nichols found pleasure and fulfillment on Tangier because it was a place where he could practice a pure kind of old-fashioned, small-town medicine. He treated everything: poison ivy and broken arms, heart disease and cancer. He sat and talked to his patients like old friends, in a sense pastoring to them, the way many physicians used to do, as he saw it, before the profession became less of a calling and more of a numbers-crunching business. He never rushed. He made house calls. He saved lives, in one way or another. Untold numbers of lives.

He and his surrogates showed up week after week, sometimes in weather so foul he had to travel by boat instead of plane, moving others to question his judgment: if the conditions were too dangerous to fly, how much safer could they have been on open water? However, they never questioned his commitment. His island patients came to trust him with their health and with the most intimate details of their lives – a hard-earned prize from such modest, private people. They baked him cakes and cookies and gave him great big hugs when they came to the clinic or when they encountered him walking the island's narrow lanes. When appointments ran late and darkness fell before he could depart for home, they would arrange their golf carts along the unlit airstrip and shine headlights so Nichols could see enough to point his plane down the runway and take off.

And now, they were praying for him. The healer was now the one who needed healing.

Since his cancer diagnosis only months earlier, Nichols could no longer pilot his own plane; his son, Davy, was at the controls this day. The disease had forced him to give up the two things he loved most aside from his family and friends: practicing medicine and flying his own aircraft. His public life had come to be defined by his service to Tangier, and becoming a pilot had provided the means to further his good work, and beyond that, well, it was just plain fun to fly. Now, both had been abruptly taken away.

After Davy guided the plane to a soft landing on the island's airstrip and taxied to a stop, Nichols exited gingerly from the aircraft. He had lost weight and strength in recent weeks, and on this visit he wore no necktie, just a V-neck sweater and light-blue shirt, perhaps the saddest signal of all that this trip was out of the ordinary. After all, you don't need to be dressed up to say goodbye. He brought along his new constant companion: a small canister of oxygen to assist his breathing. He knew each trip to his beloved Tangier might be his last, so he savored each breath of sea air, held each hug a little more tightly, laughed a little more deeply at the telling of another old story.

The streets of Tangier were quiet as the seasonal tourist boats quit running every October. As Nichols walked past the island's schoolhouse, a teacher emerged to wrap his arms around Nichols and tell him how much he cared for him. It was like that everywhere he went.

Nichols stopped for lunch at Lorraine's, the only year-round restaurant on the island. Lorraine Marshall ran the place with her daughter, Jamie Parks, who after learning of Nichols' illness had wiped her eyes and spoken for many when she said, "He's been coming since I was a little girl. I can't even describe what he's meant to all of us." Five generations of their family had been patients of Nichols. When Marshall heard he was coming for lunch, she made a pot of his favorite homemade chicken noodle soup.

"Best soup in the world," Nichols said between spoonfuls. Chicken soup? On Tangier *Island*? Despite the many years he spent coming to Tangier, Nichols never developed a taste for seafood, which he acknowledged was something of a missed opportunity in a place known for its soft-shell crabs and crab cakes. He much preferred a good hamburger or a hot dog or a fistful of M&Ms. Between handshakes and embraces, he polished off a big bowl of soup. As he ate, Ginny Marshall, Lorraine's mom, sat at his table to chat. After lunch, as Nichols left the restaurant, Lorraine Marshall handed him two tubs of soup to carry home.

Though Nichols' work on Tangier was but a fraction of his total medical practice, the island held a disproportionate grip on his heart. The islanders, he said, taught him about faith and friendship and the ability to see what's truly important in life, as they went about their lives in a place that was losing jobs, population, and most troubling, land itself. On top of that, Tangier was losing its beloved physician.

"I don't know what we'd do without him," Parks said.

These two endangered creatures – the old-fashioned country doctor and the unique little island – had clung to each other for so long, maybe without even realizing it. They had pressed forward together, determined to keep their traditions alive, against the incoming tide of time and change.

In many ways, Nichols had prepared the island for his ultimate departure. He led the drive to build a modern, sparkling health center, and he had made sure patients entering the new place were greeted by a familiar face: Inez Pruitt, the island's first homegrown, licensed medical-care provider, and of course, his protégé. She had become a physician assistant through her own hard work to be sure, but also because of Nichols' teaching, his constant encouragement and occasional badgering, and his unquestioned affection for her. Homer and Wilbur.

On this November day, Nichols walked through the door of the new clinic, and he and Pruitt embraced, as they always did. It was difficult for either to recall life without the other; 31 years earlier, she was one of his first patients, a 17-year-old newly married, high school dropout who over the years became his closest friend on the island.

As they sat in Nichols' new office, they consulted about patients, reminisced about cases and needled each other mercilessly and tenderly. They were like siblings – he the older brother, tutoring his younger sister in the ways of the family business. The love had been tough sometimes, but it was unmistakable.

"He's saved so many lives," said Pruitt. "He's just always been here – someone to depend on for strength, not only physical but spiritual and mental."

They always enjoyed poking fun at one another, and the laughter on this day was never more welcome, allowing the sad reality of the situation to remain largely unspoken. Many tears already had been shed and more surely would come, but there was a sense of comfort for everyone in knowing Nichols would never be far away, his ashes buried in the cemetery next to the health center.

In those final months, Nichols, who by his own admission was not much of a churchgoer, turned deeply introspective and examined questions of faith and after-life. As a scientist, he had always been questioning on religious matters, but as his body grew weaker his spiri-tuality grew stronger.

"He had more questions than answers," said his brother Peter. "But he wanted so much to know there is something after. He hoped there was something after. He believed in God. He knew he was fortunate to have a life's purpose and that that life's purpose came in part from good fortune and in part from God."

Dan Kraftson, a neighbor in White Stone, talked to Nichols several times over the final months about spiritual matters, the last time in December when Kraftson came to Nichols' bedside.

"He said, 'I believe in Jesus, but I just don't know if I have enough faith,' and he kind of tapped his hand to his chest," Kraftson said. "I said, 'David, God is a gracious god. Just ask him to give you that faith. It's not more complicated than receiving a gift.'

"I told David, 'This is not the end. I fully expect to see you again.'"

On Dec. 22, he sent an email to the *Richmond Times-Dispatch*, in response to a question for a follow-up story on him and his work on Tangier.

"I shall miss my friends on Tangier Island," he wrote. "I wish I could turn everything around, but I know reality is coming. I am growing weary of constant pain and markedly diminished quality of life issues and wonder what is it that I will be giving up today. All that said, I still maintain a fairly positive outlook."

The Nichols family 2010 Christmas card. (From left) Ivana and Davy, David and Dianne, Sarah and Tom. *Nichols family*

As the end grew near, Nichols was surrounded by family and friends. Dianne became principal caregiver, while Davy continued to serve as something of a "life coach" for his dad, keeping him focused on moving forward, anticipating the next day, finding something new to cross off that "bucket list" as long as he was physically able. Sarah, who lived in Delaware where she worked as a hospital administrator, would make the five-hour drive each Thursday night and spend a long weekend with her family. Her boyfriend, Tom Nagle, would often join her.

Inez Pruitt came from Tangier from time to time, and on one visit she listened, along with Dianne, Sarah and Davy, as Nichols told them how he wanted his memorial service to be conducted. First and foremost, he said, he wanted the service on Tangier, and he reiterated his wish to be buried on the island. Secondly, he wanted the service to be private; he considered the grand-opening of the health center to be his public funeral. The guest list would include family and a few friends from the mainland, and anyone from Tangier who wanted to attend. He wanted it held at Swain United Methodist, and he picked out the music. He couldn't remember the song titles, but he described the songs for Pruitt and tasked her with finding them.

Later that same day, Nichols was resting in bed. Pruitt and Tess Owens, a nurse from his practice, were with him. He took Pruitt's hand and motioned toward the French doors that revealed a view of the Rappahannock River, wide and sparkling and busy with watercraft. The doors were decorated with suncatchers, gifts from Jean and Trudy Autry, two of his Tangier patients.

"I look at these every day and look out over the Rappahannock and start to think about my departure," Nichols said. "This is where I want to be when I pass on. I believe when my spirit leaves my body it will go out through these doors, down the river, across the bay and to Tangier, paradise, and then on to my final destination, Heaven."

They all cried. "It was so beautiful," Pruitt said.

He and Bob Newman, his friend and former colleague, chatted by phone, and Newman said, "He told me he was totally satisfied with his life."

On Christmas Eve, Nagle came to Nichols' bedside and asked him for his daughter's hand in marriage and showed him the ring he planned to give her. They had a warm conversation, and on Christmas morning Nagle proposed to Sarah.

"My dad was so thrilled that we were engaged," Sarah said. "I was getting married, Davy was going to [graduate school at] William and Mary. We were going to be OK. Everything got kind of wrapped up real tightly."

Two days after Christmas, Carter and attorney B.H. Hubbard III came for a visit, bringing legal documents relating to the foundation that Nichols, though he was bedridden, wanted to see. He insisted on remaining engaged, meticulous to the end.

Hubbard first met Nichols when the young physician visited White Stone in 1979 to consider opening a practice. Hubbard's grandfather was a country doctor, and his father, mother and aunt had given the property to the town for construction of a medical office building that later was vacated and eventually became the first home for Nichols' practice. Over the years, they had become friends as Nichols became his parents' doctor and because Hubbard took flying lessons at the Topping airport. Their sons also became the best of friends.

"A very sweet time visiting with him," Hubbard re-called. "I think he just wanted to see us again. We talked a long time. He was moving slowly … but I thought he looked pretty good. At the end, he gave me a hug and Jimmie a hug. A little bit of weeping on all sides."

Recalled Carter, "He said that day was the first time he realized that death was imminent. He said, 'I'm getting ready to die.' He said he wasn't scared of dying, but he was going to miss everybody so much."

A diagnostician to the end, Nichols told Carter and Hubbard he sensed the toxins building in his body would soon overcome him and he would slide into a coma. Shortly thereafter, he did just that.

Two days later, Inez Pruitt came for one more visit along with Tess Owens. Nichols had not spoken or com-municated all day. Pruitt bent down and whispered in his ear, "You ain't purdy none" – his favorite Tangier saying, meaning "You're beautiful" – and he reached up his right hand and touched her face.

Nichols died on Dec. 30 at 6:30 a.m., peacefully, surrounded by family, as the cold morning's first light drew back a blanket of darkness from the Rappahannock, a tranquil scene unfolding just beyond Nichols' bedroom. You could see it plain as day through those suncatchers on the French doors. It was a Thursday.

Later that morning, Dianne told friends it was all so fitting that her husband passed on early on a Thursday "because that is when he always left for Tangier."

David and Dianne were married for 38 years.
Nichols family

The cemetery where Nichols' ashes are buried is next door to the David B. Nichols Health Center.
Bill Lohmann

THIRTEEN

Going Home
'It's Thursday and the doctor is in'

*O*n a cold, cloudless January morning, David Nichols made his final trip to Tangier. Fittingly, it was a Thursday. The 12th day of Christmas. Epiphany.

But this time – unlike most of his other journeys to Tangier – he went by sea, not air. The seasonal ferry from Virginia's western shore had shut down more than two months earlier, so the Courtney Thomas, the mail boat that operates year-round between Tangier and Crisfield, Md., came across the bay on a special run to pick up a small group of Nichols' family and friends in Reedville. Abiding Nichols' wishes, they headed to the island for his funeral. They carried his ashes in a small marble box.

As winter days go on the bay, this one was downright benevolent. The hour-long ride was frosty and breezy, but far from unbearable. The small party arrived on Tangier before noon, and the island was quiet, a reflection perhaps of the somber occasion but also because it was a weekday in winter, meaning no tourists. Those who knew Nichols' best would have the island to themselves to say goodbye.

Nichols had become so well-known and widely admired that a funeral on the mainland easily could have drawn hundreds, possibly thousands, along with certain media coverage. Yet he did not want a spectacle. What he wanted was a small service on the island, in Swain Memorial Church, for family, a few friends from the mainland, and the people of Tangier. Typically thorough, he selected the music and made sure food would be served after the service; the islanders arranged for a covered-dish lunch at New Testament, Tangier's other church. He didn't want the watermen to lose time from harvesting oysters to attend. "He made it clear he did not want anyone to skip work," Pruitt said. "He said he would have worked if necessary so he wanted those who needed to work to work." So, the service was scheduled for 1 p.m., late enough for the watermen to put in a full day on the job and get to the church if they wished. The island's school dismissed early.

Tangiermen paraded to the church in their golf carts, creating what passes for a traffic jam on the island, and once inside took their seats in the outer oaken pews. The front-and-center spots were reserved for those from away: Nichols' family and mainland friends and col-

leagues. The lovely old church's sanctuary, bathed in fil-
tered light streaming through its stained-glass windows,
was a sea of blue – blue jackets, blue dresses, blue neckties – in honor of Nichols. Blue was his favorite color.

The church was still decorated for Christmas,
so the poinsettias added a holiday touch to the flowers
brought in for the occasion: one arrangement came in
the shape of a helicopter, another looked like three giant M&MS: red, green and blue. Nichols loved M&Ms;
he could be bought with chocolate, his friends said. The
marble box rested nearby.

Swain's pastor, the Rev. Patricia Stover, presided
over the service. Solos were sung by Jean Crockett and
Jared Parks, who was intricately connected to Nichols
through his wife (Anna Pruitt-Parks), mother (Cindy
Parks) and mother-in-law (Inez Pruitt). It was so Tangier.
It was so right.

Jimmie Carter, who like several other close friends
and family members in attendance wore neckties bor-
rowed from Nichols' closet, spoke and joked about his
friend's love of hamburgers, well-done, at Lorraine's and
the way he loved to be called David Nichols Parks. "The
only thing he loved in this life more than Tangier was his
family," said Carter, who had become so close to David
in his later years that he became known as the fifth Nichols brother. "Never have I seen a man love a place so
strongly. He's going to be so happy here."

Peter Nichols offered a moving eulogy, thanking the people of Tangier for giving his brother a sense of himself and a sense of what's important in life. He recalled a few weeks earlier when David needed treatment at a North Carolina hospital for respiratory problems and even then, despite his pain, was more concerned about others.

"He was asking the doctor and the nurses, whom he'd never met before, about themselves," Peter Nichols said. "He wanted to know where they were from, what they thought, what was important to them. The biggest thing I'll remember about David in the last little while was his incredible gentle grace."

No matter how you knew David, Peter said, you knew David.

"You know what David gave his patients as a doctor: the time, the listening, the asking questions and caring about the answers, the looking you straight in the eye, the wanting to know how you feel," he said. "That's the same way he was with his friends. That's the same way he was with his brothers. The same way."

He ended with a prayer written many years earlier by their mother.

Faith can be a fragile thing
But so are the bones in a seagull's wings

If they carry him high o'er the stormy sea
Dear Lord let my faith do that for me

Then Inez Pruitt, a.k.a. Homer, stood.

"It's Thursday," she said, "and the doctor is in."

Pruitt said the sort of things she always said when she talked about the man who had gone from being her physician to her boss to her mentor to her friend.

"He had a gift, and the gift was he was like a light," she said. "He had a way of making people feel and believe without a shadow of a doubt they were where they were supposed to be.

"There were many people behind Dr. Nichols. Nothing he did was alone. He had a way of bringing out the best in people. He had the gift of seeing the potential in other people and encouraging them to dream the dream … and he knew how to pick a team of players who could work together."

She invoked a prayer written by John Henry Cardinal Newman – that Nichols wanted in the service.

From their movie "The Cider House Rules:"

"Oh, Lord, support us all the day long, until the shadows lengthen and the evening comes, and the busy world is hushed, and the fever of life is over, and our

work is done. Then, in thy mercy grant us a safe lodging and a holy rest, and peace at the last."

She wasn't finished with the movie references.

"To Wilbur," she said, "Good night you prince of White Stone and Tangier, you king of Virginia."

When the service was over, Davy and Sarah Nichols took the marble box containing their father's ashes and led the mourners outside to the cemetery next door. They stopped at a freshly open plot under a green funeral canopy rippling in the chilly breeze. A few words were said, a prayer was spoken, and then family and friends walked up, one by one, and tenderly offered their last gifts – single, long-stem roses – to the man who had given the island so much.

So there, behind the white picket fence, in the first row of graves closest to the David B. Nichols Health Center, David B. Nichols was home, among the Crocketts and the Pruitts, and yes, the Parks. In the end, a true Tangierman.

Nichols' gravestone in the Tangier cemetery memorializes his flying and his service to the island. *Nichols family*

Nichols during an interview in the old Tangier clinic in August 2010.
Bob Brown/Richmond Times-Dispatch.

AFTERWORD

A mainland celebration of life was held at Hummel Field Airport for Nichols four months after his death. More than 300 people gathered, seated in folding chairs in the hangar where he normally kept his plane and helicopter. He was eulogized by family and friends, colleagues and business associates, remembered not only for his work with patients in White Stone and on Tangier but for the way he carried himself around his neighborhood.

One of the speakers was Linda Menzer, a friend and neighbor, who first noticed David while he was on his regular morning runs, heading toward his turnaround point: a giant oak tree.

"His great big smile was all I knew about him at first," she said. "His energy reminded me of a young boy at play."

She came to know him, she said, as someone who led his life the same way: "With energy and enthusiasm that just wouldn't quit.

"David didn't live his life small," she said. "He lived it with a presence and a power that liberated others."

At that service, Scott Nichols remembered his brother as "an uncommonly decent man."

He also was an uncommonly prepared man who did not like leaving things to chance. It was his nature as a physician and as a businessman to be thorough, to consider all possibilities, to relentlessly pursue the best deal, whether the matter at hand was a patient's diagnosis or a real estate investment. He was not one to sit back and let circumstances dictate his destiny. He never wanted to forget anything that needed doing, which is why he kept unceasing to-do lists on legal pads. He would cross off items as he (or someone else) completed them and just add new ones to the bottom, until he filled the pad. Then, according to his daughter, Sarah, he would archive the pad in case he needed to refer it to it later and start a new list on a fresh pad.

"We probably have those from the last 20 years," she said.

He refused to allow himself to lose sight of what needed to be done, although maintaining control was only part of his purpose; achieving the ultimate desired outcome was always his aim. He was quite happy for others to do the work, in fact he often preferred it, but he wanted to make certain they knew precisely the work they were supposed to do.

Even as his health failed in the final months and days of his life, Nichols endeavored to cross off the remaining items on his to-do list. A major objective was ensuring quality medical care for the residents of Tangier long after he was gone. He had done that in big ways by bringing the island into his practice and by mentoring Inez Pruitt, who would be on the island every day, and when it came time to sell his lucrative practice by finding a buyer – Riverside Medical Group – willing to take on Tangier. But there was another piece that remained unresolved: adequate health insurance coverage for the islanders.

Because of their relatively low incomes, a significant number of Tangiermen were eligible for government assistance, but many had never been able to navigate the maze of paperwork required to gain that help. Many, too, were self-employed, which complicated proving eligibility. Rather than waging bureaucratic battle, many islanders found it easier just to make do without insurance coverage. The problem was some islanders resisted seeking treatment they needed because of a lack of insurance, while others found themselves swimming in debt because of hefty medical bills – not bills from Nichols' practice but from mainland specialists and hospitals.

After his cancer diagnosis, Nichols went to Iris Treakle and asked her to help Tangier. Nichols had known Treakle for years. They met decades earlier at Rappahannock General Hospital, where Treakle was a 19-year-old operating room technician and Nichols was a young physician in the community building his practice. She later operated a cleaning business in the White Stone area, mostly for professional offices, and Nichols' practice was one of those clients. Her son grew up a patient of the practice, and though she was rarely sick, Treakle sought out Nichols on occasional personal medical issues. She later became an independent insurance agent specializing in health insurance. She recalled "big conversations" about insurance with Nichols as they discussed health insurance coverage for his staff. Treakle also was a recreational runner who would bump into Nichols on her workouts around town. "How many miles have you been this morning, Iris?" he would say as they passed.

"It was really neat how we got to know each other," she said.

Nichols had watched Treakle grow from a young hospital employee into a confident, well-respected businesswoman. He clearly liked what he saw – the way she worked so hard, her enthusiastic approach to everything she did, the manner in which she helped people, including himself, understand something as complicated as health insurance. He envisioned Treakle as someone else he could bring aboard his Tangier bandwagon.

"I need you to go to Tangier and do what you do here," she recalled Nichols telling her. He told her many of the islanders needed help wading through the bureaucratic red tape. They were set as far as medical care, but the widespread lack of insurance coverage was a major concern. He wanted to make certain nothing would jeopardize what so many had worked for as far as medical care for the island. The people of Tangier needed a caring, knowledgeable advocate.

"You're the link that's missing," he told her.

"Oh my goodness!" Treakle thought. "How am I going to do that?"

But she told him she would, and then she figured out how. Nichols, apparently, knew she would. Before she could start meeting the islanders and helping them, Treakle underwent hundreds of hours of training to become educated about the various insurance plans offered by the state of Virginia, such as FAMIS (Family Access to Medical Insurance Security), the low-cost health insurance for children of working parents.

Three weeks before he died, a weakened Nichols visited Treakle to see how the training was going and to make sure she would follow through.

"He sat at my desk and said, 'You promise me you're going?'" Treakle recalled Nichols asking her. "I said, 'I promise you I'm going, and I'll do anything I can.'

"I will never forget what he said: 'Go to Tangier, and you will shine!'"

And she did.

A year after Nichols' death, after she had completed all of her training, Treakle began making weekly visits to Tangier, all as an unpaid volunteer. Davy Nichols would fly her over every Tuesday, then return to fetch her the next day. She met with islanders as a group, explaining what Nichols had asked her to do, and then she began consulting with them one-by-one, working through their individual situations, gradually earning their trust. When she started, Treakle estimated 75 percent of islanders younger than 65 did not have health insurance, and less than one-quarter of the children were insured. Within a year, all of the previously uninsured were covered.

She not only came to understand Nichols' love of Tangier, but she began to love it, too. She spearheaded a community effort to build a house for a family whose uninsured home was destroyed in a fatal fire. On summer Sundays, she and her family started taking the Reedville ferry to the island, carrying fresh vegetables from their farm to share with Tangier residents, another of Nichols' wishes: to improve their access to fresh produce.

It was uncanny how whenever a problem arose, Treakle jumped in to start finding a solution. For her work on Tangier, Treakle was named an Unsung Hero in 2013 as a "child health champion" by the Virginia Health Care Foundation, and she directed her $2,000 prize to the Tangier health center.

"Iris is a hero here," said Inez Pruitt, who is looked upon by many in the same way.

Jimmie Carter, founder and president of the Tangier Health Foundation and executive director of the Rappahannock General Hospital Foundation, said Treakle is "following in the footsteps of Dr. Nichols and Inez."

"It's just amazing what she's been able to do," Carter said. "David had a way of really empowering people."

It's difficult to tell how much Nichols empowered people and how much he simply gravitated toward good people who could get the work done. In 2013, Carter was honored as the Senior Volunteer of the Year by the Governor's Office on Volunteerism and Community Service. He was cited for his work on behalf of a variety of causes, most notably improving the delivery of health care in rural, underserved communities, including Tangier. That same year, Inez Pruitt was among eight women recognized by the Library of Virginia as part of its Virginia Women in History program.

Even after he was gone, Nichols' legendary ability to teach and delegate and get people to do things beyond their own expectations – and perhaps even more impressive, get others to share his passion for his work – lived on. Treakle has devoted untold hundreds of hours of her own time to help Tangier, a place she barely knew before Nichols asked for her help. To an outsider, it might make little sense. To Treakle, it makes perfect sense. "He asked me to," she said of her motivation, "and I know I can do it."

But she can't help but wonder:

"How did he know this?" she said. "How did this man know I would go over and do the things I've done? I believe with all my heart that Dr. Nichols is their guardian angel."

In September 2014, the Aircraft Owners and **Pilots Association** honored Nichols' memory by erecting a pair of identical monuments; one at Hummel Field and the other at the health center on Tangier. AOPA, the largest aviation association in the world, had long followed and been supportive of Nichols' work .

"It's just a great story, " said Mark Baker, AOPA's president and chief executive officer, who attended both ceremonies and piloted one of the planes that ferried Nichols' family and friends to Tangier for the event. "We've used it as a valuable community-building story over and over. People get inspired by it ... how to use (aviation) in a positive way."

The monuments were created from the same piece of granite by Richmond's A.P. Grappone & Sons Inc. Each bears the title: "Dr. Copter - Flying Medicine To Tangier."

Inez Pruitt recalled Nichols had always told her, "No monument, the clinic is my monument."

But what would he think now?

"He'd eat it up," she said with a laugh.

The Nichols home in White Stone has a name, Park Place, and its origin is, yes, the popular game of Monopoly. "It was one of David's favorite games," said Dianne Nichols, "and this property looked like a park. It just seemed to fit." It has brick columns in the front at the entrance to the long driveway that leads you to the fine house on four acres. There is a brick helicopter pad in the front yard, a swimming pool on the side and in the back, with tall pines scattered along the bank of the Rappahannock, an exquisite view of the river.

Inside, Dianne sorted through scrapbooks of newspaper and magazine stories about her late husband. She showed me the hallway between the kitchen and the entry foyer where there were framed photographs, resolutions, commendations and letters – including one from

President George W. Bush and another from Virginia Gov. Tim Kaine – on display. The "Wall of Wonder," she called it. She said her husband enjoyed the recognition.

"Everybody likes a pat on the back," she said.

We went through many of his papers, as well as boxes and albums of cards, letters and photos, his old pilot logbooks, the years of calendars she meticulously kept to help make sure David and the rest of the family got where they needed to be. She mentioned how in the early days – before computers and mobile phones – David was "tethered, literally, to the phone in the kitchen. He couldn't go on the boat. He'd have to be here to answer the phone." In his final years, he made good use of his cell phone – with the extra battery pack – as he'd take it with him everywhere he went: to meetings of the various boards he served on, on early-morning walks or weekend visits to undeveloped fields to scout possible real estate investments.

"I don't know how David did everything he did," she said.

In fact, to those who know the family, it was the loving support of Dianne through the years that largely enabled David to do all he did.

Left - A pair of identical monuments honoring Nichols were dedicated in September 2014 at Hummel Field Airport in Topping and here at the David B. Nichols Health Center on Tangier Island. The monuments, each bearing the words "Dr. Copter – Flying Medicine To Tangier," were created from the same piece of granite by Richmond's A.P. Grappone & Sons Inc. and were gifts from the Aircraft Owners and Pilots Association (AOPA), the largest aviation association in the world that had long followed and supported Nichols' work.
Bill Lohmann

There were the regular flights to Tangier, but David's flying enabled numerous family trips to destinations including the Bahamas, Walt Disney World and Newfoundland. No matter where he went, he found people to talk to, which was interesting for a man viewed by some as quiet and reserved. He simply didn't like to talk about himself. He was fine asking others about themselves, so much so that his daughter, Sarah, recalled with a laugh that she used to be afraid to bring home boyfriends "because I was afraid he would grill them."

"My dad had an appreciation for connecting with people who were very salt-of-the-earth," she said. "We were part of a country club for a couple of years … but it just wasn't him. He wasn't a schmoozer by any means. He did not like going to cocktail parties or putting on airs. He loved Tangier. No airs on Tangier at all."

I asked if that is why he felt so comfortable there.

"Exactly," she said.

Sarah and Tom married a year after her father's death, and in 2013 she gave birth to their son, Truman. In 2016, they welcomed a daughter, Juliet. Sarah is vice president of strategy and planning for Christiana Care Health System in Delaware. In talking about her dad, Sarah noted there was a warmth to him that outsiders might not have seen. "He was a very loving, supportive father and my biggest cheerleader," she said.

In another family addition since Nichols' death, Davy and his wife, Ivana, had a daughter, June, born in March 2014.

After his father's passing, Davy earned a master of business administration degree from the College of William and Mary, something his father greatly encouraged him to do. "Partly," Davy said, "because I think he had a few medical buddies that had done it later in life and really enjoyed the experience. Perhaps he wanted to do it himself, or perhaps he was 'preparing' me for taking over his many businesses and financial affairs." Classes started less than two weeks after his father died, but the quick turnaround was, as Davy put it, "a blessing in disguise."

"Had I stayed in White Stone, I would have been surrounded by people that knew Dad, constant reminders of his loss," he said. "The MBA and 34 new friends were my escape and absolutely perfectly timed."

His academic pursuit, Davy said, "re-ignited my spirit."

Davy now flies to Tangier several times a week, ferrying people and supplies to the island. He is the facility manager for the Tangier Health Foundation, meaning he is the property manager, maintenance man and chief pilot, flying Riverside physicians to Tangier on a weekly basis. In addition, he took his father's place on the foundation's board. . He also operates Buell Bay Co., the company formed by his father that owns the hangar and plane, and he's also started a new company, Coastal Sky Taxi, a commercial charter operation. Davy jokes that he always feels a little closer to his dad when he's flying because of the altitude, but there are other reasons, too.

"I can remember flying with him as some of my earliest memories," Davy said. "I remember after each landing, he'd put me on his lap and let me turn the yoke back and forth like I was steering. I thought it was nuts. When I was old enough, he broke the news that while taxiing, you steer with your feet on the rudder pedals. It was like learning that Santa was not real!

"I remember accidentally opening the window at 10,000 feet flying over St. John's Bay on the way to Newfoundland as a toddler. That got everyone's heart pumping. I remember always listening to him communicate on the radio and asking a million questions. Dad and I both were hard of hearing, but in the plane we were both crystal clear because of the headsets. Many of our deepest conversations were while flying long distances where there was little to do but talk. I guess you could say every time I get in the plane I think of Dad and his voice saying things like 'Don't forget to turn off the master switch.' I think he's up there, keeping me safe, keeping an eye on me, and sometimes I think he's still sitting next to me. Probably silently rating how smooth my landings are and nodding in approval. Or if I have a bouncer of a landing, he's probably saying, 'Whoa, which one of those landings are you going to count? The first bounce or the second?!'"

In 2018, Dianne continued to live at the home she and David built on the Rappahannock, and said she couldn't imagine moving from the river any time soon.

On Tangier, the fight goes on to save the vanishing island. Residents await construction of the long-planned jetty at the mouth of the channel leading into the island's harbor and hope political leaders will rally behind their cause with the necessary funding.

Born in 1945, John I. Pruitt grew up on Tangier, left to go to college, became a newspaper reporter and editor, and still lives away, though he has family on the island and has always been a regular visitor. By not living on the island but returning frequently with his wife and other family members -- often three generations -- he also has noticed the island's incremental decline. He was reminded of that during a 2014 visit when he went into the marsh on the island where he keeps a small skiff.

"I waded from what was my grandfather's house to the boat," said Pruitt, who retired after a career across the bay at The Virginian-Pilot in Norfolk. "When I was a child, we played high and dry in the very marsh that I waded in.

"To me, it's dismaying how quickly things are evolving. I knew Tangier was not going to last forever unless something was done about the erosion, but there isn't enough money around to protect Tangier totally."

And it pains him to say: "Seawall or not, Tangier is not sustainable. The water level of the bay is rising, the land level of Tangier is declining. You become a soup bowl."

In retirement, Pruitt founded Tangier Pride, an organization that emphasized "self-help," as Pruitt put it, "to encourage the island to address the issues it can address." Like litter control. Pruitt organizes clean-up days and helps raise money for projects such as placing trash receptacles around Tangier.

"The whole idea that I keep in mind is, 'We don't have long, so let's make the island the best," he said. The house where Pruitt grew up flooded four times in three years – if he remembers correctly – and eventually had to be razed. On visits, he stays at another home on the property. He relishes an uncommon comfort on Sunday mornings looking up at the Swain Memorial choir and seeing faces he recognizes from his childhood.

"We love going," he said. "There's such a rich heritage there. Little kids have little boats, sort of miniatures that their dads have built for them. They go out in those ditches and crab as seriously as their dads are out in the bay.

"I have a little boat, and I putt around the ditches. It's sort of reliving childhood, I suppose, but it's so pleasant and soothing to be out there. In the night, there is not a sound to be heard. You're out far enough and you can look at the sky. It's just a beautiful place."

In July 2016, Tangier received a nice boost when it was announced that it had been chosen to become part of the Virginia Oyster Trail, a public-private partnership that highlights locations around coastal Virginia where oysters are harvested. The trail features restaurants, lodging and art venues – as well as the oysters themselves – in an effort to promote the oyster business and attract visitors. Virginia First Lady Dorothy McAuliffe traveled to Tangier to make the announcement. Her husband, Gov. Terry McAuliffe, likes to say, "The oyster is to Virginia what lobster is to Maine."

"A banner day on Tangier," said Anna Pruitt-Parks, a member of the island's town council. "We love our Tangier Sound oysters and feel that they are some of the best in the world, and we are finally glad to see them getting the recognition that they deserve!"

Oysters take on the flavors of the waters in which they grow, and oysters of the Tangier region – according to a brochure from the Virginia Marine Products Board – offer a flavor "with a balance of salt and sweet, and a savory butter/cream finish."

The story goes beyond mere taste for Tangier. Pruitt-Parks said the economic impact of being part of the oyster trail is important to the island. She hopes oysters, as well as oyster aquaculture, "will be a huge part of the future of Tangier Island."

Wild oysters are on the rebound throughout the bay after poor harvests in the 1980s and 1990s. Oysters produced by aquaculture also are on the rise, and Tangier Island Oyster Co. is representative of that trend. The aqua-farming operation is financed by a group of investors – many from the Richmond area who have a lifelong family connection and love for the bay – who consider themselves "social investors." Their aim is to do well in the oyster business and do good by Tangier.

"We started the company to help secure Tangier's place in the world, to draw attention to its cultural value and uniqueness," said Tim Hickey, a writer who grew up in Richmond and was among those who came up with the idea.

The company has set up scores of floating oyster cages tethered to seabed anchors in the open waters of Tangier Sound to take advantage of the nutrient-rich surface waters of the bay, launching in 2013 and investing almost a half-million dollars into the enterprise in the first three years. The company lost most of its cages in a February 2015 winter storm, but replaced the lost cages and pressed on. Its first harvested oysters were well-received by chefs along the East Coast.

Those who started the company have invested a lot of sweat equity in the project, but they have hired Tangier watermen to tend to the oysters as they grow. Manager Craig Suro, the lead entrepreneur behind the project, said the company hopes to work with more watermen from the island as the operation expands.

Suro's friend and fellow investor, Baylor Rice, said he's been visiting the bay since he was a child. He said he loves the bay, and he loves that each oyster filters up to 50 gallons of water a day.

"So, this is a way I can help the bay ... while helping the people of Tangier," he said. "And at the end of the day, if we can make a profit on it, that's a fantastic thing."

Tangier's population has dropped in recent decades. According to the 2010 U.S. census – and subsequent updated estimates – the island's population is more than 700. However, Tangier officials say the actual population is less than 500 as Tangiermen increasingly have left the island for jobs.

At Tangier Combined School enrollment stood over 100 at the turn of the 21st century. By the 2017-18 academic year, however, the enrollment had fallen to 61, with a senior class of six, said school principal Nina Pruitt.

Overall, the Tangier population is aging. By 2014, the median age on Tangier was 54.8, compared to 37.9 across the United States, according to the U.S. Census.

As the population dropped, a one-time housing shortage on the island turned into a glut. Marilyn Pruitt, an office assistant in the town office, recalled the housing shortage on the island when she got married in 1992.

"We couldn't even find a place to live," she said. "There was nothing available."

In the summer of 2015, she counted 70 to 75 unoccupied houses on the island. By the summer of 2016, that number had dropped into the 60s, said then-town manager Renee Tyler, with the arrival of several new families, including Jerry and Rebecca Dunivan and their five children (and two goats) from a farm in suburban Richmond. They were drawn by the wholesome environment on the island – a place "with a little bit more of a slow pace," said Rebecca – and purchased a home across the street from Spanky's ice cream parlor.

"It's like a big family here, and yeah, there are family squabbles and everybody knows your business," she said, "but at the same time, if there's ever a crisis, everyone is going to come out of the woodwork [to help]. It reminds me of what I imagined the 1950s to be like."

She and her husband found plenty of work to make a living – finishing drywall, installing floors, roofing, plumbing and welding and even repairing golf carts. She didn't sound particularly worried about moving to what is said to be a disappearing island. She believed something would be done to save Tangier.

"I don't think we're going to disappear," she said. "If it did, it would be a crime. The way of life here is so unique. I plan on living here the rest of my life."

Almost eight years after Nichols' death, the David B. Nichols Health Center remains a gem. Riverside Medical Group flies in physicians every week, often Thursdays, just as Nichols and his colleagues did for more than 30 years, and just as Riverside had promised when Nichols sold the practice. The Riverside doctors serve as supervising physicians – in person or by phone – to Pruitt, who is at the health center every day, tending to her neighbors' needs.

"Inez is really the rock," Carter said. "She's the 24/7 medical provider."

Medical care on the island has never been better, and the future of healthcare on the island is bright. Pruitt said the center "outshines" almost every other medical facility she visits because of the advanced equipment available to her and her nurses. The endowment set up during fundraising for the construction not only pays for upkeep at the health center, but also finances scholarships to encourage graduates of the Tangier Combined School to pursue careers in the medical field. In addition, Carter said, endowment funds could be used to help secure a replacement for Inez Pruitt whenever she steps away from the job.

For now, though, the job is all Pruitt wants. She pursues the work every day with Nichols in her mind and in her heart.

"Still miss him greatly," Pruitt said. "He was such a teacher."

Yet, Pruitt said of Nichols, she still feels his presence.

"Sometimes when I've got a difficult case, it's almost like I hear him whispering in my ear," she said.

She had occasion to have dinner with a physician assistant from the mainland whose work she admires and operates in high-pressure circumstances – and the upshot of their conversation was that he marveled at what *she* does on Tangier.

"He said, 'I wouldn't be you for anything in the world, living on an isolated island and running a clinic on your own,'" Pruitt recalled. "I don't think about it. It's just what Dr. Nichols taught us to do. We were just told to do your job and do it to the best of your ability – and then some."

That "then some" included doing something in the summer of 2015 that Nichols never did during his time on Tangier: deliver a baby. (Although Nichols delivered numerous babies on the mainland, including his own son.) Pruitt said she had put the mom-to-be in an ambulance headed for the island's airport and a flight to a Maryland hospital — but the baby wouldn't wait. The baby was delivered in the ambulance.

"The baby was fine, a beautiful baby girl," Pruitt said. "It was very exciting. I was on Cloud Nine for several days."

But the never-a-dull-moment nature of her work keeps her grounded. She told of treating a 3-year-old boy with a dislocated elbow.

"Nichols would have fixed that in no time," she said, "but I don't have that much training in orthopedics."

So she was put in touch with a physician on the mainland who assured her he was confident she could return the elbow to its proper alignment with his instructions over the phone – just the way Nichols had done so many times in so many cases.

"The doctor talked me through it," she said, "and the thing popped right in place."

She added with a laugh, "All I could think of was that Wilbur would have been so proud."

He also likely would be proud of the way, years later, Pruitt occasionally signed her emails:

"Inez (still AKA Homer)."

AUTHOR'S NOTE

*T*he reporting and writing of this book began in 2010 and proceeded off and on for eight years before coming to fruition. I conducted dozens of interviews with members of Dr. David Nichols' family, his colleagues and patients, and others who know Tangier from a historical or scientific perspective. I also gleaned information from old newspaper and magazine stories and books about Tangier, which I've credited by attribution within the text. The Tangier History Museum on the island also was a great source of information.

I'm grateful to all who helped with this project, particularly members of David's family – his widow, Dianne, daughter, Sarah, and son, Davy, and his brothers – who were exceedingly helpful and patient (and many thanks to Davy Nichols for occasional flights to the island). I'm indebted to the people of Tangier for inviting me into their homes and for generously sharing their stories.

I'm also appreciative for the assistance of the Tangier Island Health Foundation and its founder and president, Jimmie Carter, without whom this book would not have become a reality.

I'm thankful for the friendship of photographer Bob Brown, my longtime colleague at the Richmond Times-Dispatch and my traveling companion on so many assignments on the back roads of Virginia. Our ambition, we always say, is to stay out of the office as much as possible, and I'd have to say we have succeeded. My friends and former newspaper colleagues, Tom Kapsidelis and Tom Mullen, were willing sounding boards throughout the project, offering encouragement and sage advice along the way. I'm also most appreciative to *The Times-Dispatch* for permission to use many of the photos in this book, and in particular to newsroom archivist Nicole Kappatos for her help.

Finally, as with anything I've ever done, I could not have completed this project without the love and support of my family, particularly my wife, Robin, who provided not only encouragement but editorial support, and my daughter Alex, who edited the manuscript into its final form.

Thank you all.

Bill Lohmann

ABOUT THE AUTHOR

*B*ill Lohmann is an award-winning reporter and columnist for the *Richmond Times-Dispatch*. He also has reported for United Press International in Richmond, Orlando and Atlanta, and began his career as a sports writer for *The Charlottesville Daily Progress*. This is his fifth book.

Bill Lohmann.
Dean Hoffmeyer/Richmond Times-Dispatch